INTO THE FURTHER REACHE

an anthology of Contemporary British Poetry
celebrating the spiritual journey

edited and introduced by Jay Ramsay

INTO THE FURTHER REACHES

an anthology of Contemporary British Poetry
celebrating the spiritual journey

edited and introduced by Jay Ramsay

PS AVALON
Glastonbury, England

First published in the U.K. in 2007 by PS Avalon

PS Avalon
Box 1865, Glastonbury
Somerset, BA6 8YR, U.K.

www.psavalon.com

cover photo: Lara Fiedler
ozphiz@onetel.com

design: Will Parfitt

ISBN 978-0-9552786-1-7

Contents

Dedication

for my father Donald – 'we are all on a journey' – and my fiancée Lara

Kathleen, Gabriel, Ann, Richard, Aidan

and with gratitude to Will Parfitt, publisher

Defence of poetry thus means: defence of humanity, defence of authenticity, it means defence of the stone against plaster, defence of wood against plastic, defence of the word of the mother tongue against the foreign word, the technical jargon, defence of feeling against hypocrisy and finally defence of everything real and true against the fashion of the day and intentional lies.

– Galsan Tschinag, *Defence of Poetry 1999: Defence of the Stone Against Plaster*

For Time, the bringer
Of abundant days
Is Time the destroyer—
In the Iron Age
The Kali Yuga
To whom can we pray
At the end of an era
But the Lord Shiva
The Liberator, the purifier ?

– Kathleen Raine, *Millennial Hymn to the Lord Shiva*

We may dwell in the house of language, but light shines through the windows from afar and we can see another world beyond the walls.

– Peter Marshall, *Riding the Wind—a new philosophy for a new era*

Introduction

An appalling world indeed is presented to us as 'real', as the late Kathleen Raine put it in her essay 'Poetry and the Frontiers of Consciousness'[1]. An informed anthology of poetry at this time is bound to be by definition apocalyptic, whether or not you believe in the Mayan Calendar (which dates the end of time to 2012, now just a few years away). For those who prefer the weather, we have climate change: melting glaciers, unstable temperatures, and hurricanes. Apocalypse: global *nigredo*: its socio-political insanity portrayed as reality, its alchemy and deeper invitation inescapable. Poets, as the living antennae of society, can't but help mirror it—so (here) we have Abbs' Dante, in an Inferno poised between then and now, Burns' 'The aeon lies torn in pieces...', and Donaldson's 'This England'. No spiritually-minded poet can ignore the fact that whatever the future holds these *are* the Last Days (as Jill Haas in her long poem states it); the world as we know it is coming to an end, and that as Kathleen was fond of saying to me 'what is to come must be something very different' (she wasn't sure how poetry as we know it could even be a part of it).

At the same time what we can (and must, I believe) also see is a negativity we can fall into that becomes part of the problem, and to which large swathes of 20th Century literature ironically testify. I call it 'Swift's Fallacy', the same trap that most satirical writers since also end up falling into—their own *mauvais foi* (bad faith). As Shakespeare warned us long ago in a line that could have been addressed to the last century 'Nothing will come of nothing. Think again'. Well, we are thinking: those of us who realize that our most worthwhile thoughts transcend the intellect, social realism and its rationalizations, and a level of linguistic conceptualization where poets become incomprehensible islands of private utterance glossed by technology.

Not the 64 Contemporary British Poets gathered here, all of whom write with transparency: none of who believe that poetry is only made of words. 'In the beginning was the Word': surely everybody knows the Word was more than a collection of letters written on a page, but apparently not. And without an actively spiritual point of view, all we have is 'language', is poetics, like smoke gathering under a ceiling. And it feels increasingly irrelevant and retro, as Andrew Staniland pointed out to me.

What can we see beyond ? There are various areas being indicated here as we travel into the further reaches; walking literal or imaginal roads into a new dawn, a reborn awareness. They come from the unconscious, that fertile as well as uncertain, mercurial ground which is also the superconscious seen in its wholeness—our antennae quivering for the whispers where poems begin. Flashes of insight through lived or witnessed experience, read in the Book of Nature, sometimes via the printed word. The consciousness that everything that is literal is also (at the same time) symbolic, More Than itself. Moments of conversation with friends where grace becomes apparent and we remember we are beings of intelligent love on a journey of reconnection and return.

Renewal, here, through being part of the earth, through our creatureliness as Karen Eberhardt Shelton passionately witnesses in her dreaming that is healing our rootlessness, restoring our sense of self. 'Only connect' as E.M. Forster famously summarized it. I can still hear my English teacher saying it. We cannot really be in life if we are living somewhere half outside it in our heads. As Mongolian shaman and poet Galsan Tschinag asserts[2]:

> *When it comes to poetry, it is necessary to ask the essential questions of life. Which are these ? They concern the beginning and the end, birth and death. And therefore I want to know: where do I come from ? Where do I go ? In nomadic terms, it is about the roots, and eventually the fruits. Roots can be geographical-spatial, historical-temporal and cultural-religious, but for us they are above all fateful, meant to be our destiny. Fruits can be children, deeds, words.*

> *Which mountain's stone am I, which well's water, which steppe's grass ? The sooner and more definitely I find an answer to this, the clearer will be the poetry which flows from me.*

Ruth Marshall's celebration of place as well as occasion echoes this both in time, and timelessly—the past poignantly and invisibly alive in the wild places also memorably gestured by Alyson Hallett in Ronald Duncan's old hut at Welcombe, North Devon, that stretch of wrecker's coast. Meanwhile Cora Greenhill's celebration of the heart and community extends this into the sacrament of our daily lives where we most need it, beyond the emptiness and boredom, the meaningless routines, the crap that is on TV and in our personality-ridden media—the fast food that nourishes nobody. As another British poet in exile, Georgina Johnson (in Israel), testifies to by contrast: the intelligent love that restores our dignity as well as our passion, in what we're here to make together in the temple of our bodies.

Galsan Tschinag goes on to say:

> *Poetry is an enormous counter-force against the oppressing weight of the material world. It is a spice in everyday life, a sting against habit, it changes life, which is more and more outweighed by consumption. Poetry, after all, belongs to the side of the heart in opposition to the stomach...*
>
> *With those people who have an overfed stomach, poetry has a hard time. Like our inner parts, so are our thoughts. From disturbed, dulled thoughts springs disturbed, weakened poetry. The reduction of poetry to decoration, as part of consumption, chopped-up prose, the unimaginative, pathetic play with form, the shameless, shallow pomposity about truism, the stringing together of sentences that are grammatically correct but cold and dead in their structure—a pseudo poetry, produced on a massive scale almost like shoes, hamburgers and non-returnable bottles, but with one decisive consequence: it annoys the readers and kills their feeling for poetry.*

His devastating analysis echoing what every one of the contributors gathered here would endorse in their own way, although perhaps not as forthrightly, numbed as we sometimes are by years of marginalization and rejection in favour of something closer to fiction than lyricism, something distinctly un-poetic, written (so it appears) by frustrated novelists and journalists, would-be philosophers immured in passé existentialism. All very strange, but all (after all) part of an exhausted age which has run out of everything except its own greying individualistic adolescence. How one longs for those 'other rooms' evoked by Rupert Loydell in praise of Peter Redgrove, those spaces of true creative magic and regained mystery.

Perhaps there is a polarity here too among the men and the women which points to a deeper and broader undercurrent—the male poets more overtly apocalyptic, concerned with the 'bigger picture', and 'descending' where the women are more obviously involved in the locality and community of life and living, 'ascending'...as well as locked somewhere together in an invisible embrace, gesturing towards a faith which transcends gender, inwardly as well as outwardly, and with a timeless and very contemporary flame (Diana Durham, Gabriel Millar, Kenneth Steven and Philip Wells come immediately to mind). The sense of the poet as above all a spiritual and human person is what emerges, perhaps just in the nick of time, beyond political fashion and egoic narcissism, re-entering the birthright of our created lives in a world that is reeling from the impact of our ignorance, a strange Red parting Sea, and a path that is leading, well... no one quite knows where.

So this anthology, my fourth, is a book for travellers on every level, and as I emphasized in inviting the poets to contribute: not only in thinking about our journey through life, but in expanding our sense of life through movement, regaining our aliveness—as Aidan Andrew Dun also witnesses so superbly, in epic mode. To move, to be moveable, to re-enter the mystery and sacredness of life and witness that with poetry seemed to me to be the best context for a new anthology, perhaps even for poetry itself. In that, it's been a special pleasure to gather old and new companions and fellow pilgrims of truth, seeing and affirming the community we are increasingly a part of with each other. At the same time, I've abandoned a specific sequence for all the material on this occasion, wanting the poems (and their authors) to speak individually for themselves—hence the mainly alphabetic arrangement, with thanks to Richard Burns. All the poets here are part of a vanguard where the great change is coming, and we will all be awake to the journey we are on. I hope these poems extend your horizons, as well as your appetite for the adventure of your life. The rest is the journey. Beyond what we may already know, or see. This is where the poetry begins. In all its fine intensity of feeling. In all its deeper, further opening. Read on.

Jay Ramsay

1 essay written/first published in 1985, as part of her work with Temenos
2 from Defence of Poetry 1999; Defence of the Stone against Plaster, transl. Kathrin Lang

The Poems

Peter Abbs

THREE POEMS SOMEWHAT AFTER DANTE'S INFERNO

IN THE THIRD CIRCLE

So we entered the third circle. Acid rain hammered down.
Hailstones and snow drove through the air, implacable –
a constant pressure. And where the flakes settled the earth stank

as if infected. Then charging through the cold black slime
I saw the three-headed dog, Cerberus. With claws unleashed
it lunged at the bewildered bodies that floundered there.

When the beast saw us it opened its three mouths so wide
I could see the jagged fangs - its breath so rank it made me retch.
My guide said nothing. Instead he bent down and with both hands

scooped up the reeking mud and rammed a handful down each throat...
As a savage mongrel settles when thown a shank of lamb
so on the instant this yapping fiend turned silent. Without a pause

we ran over the living corpses, our feet touching lightly
their sunken limbs and would have made our escape but for one
who cried out: *Oh you who glide through this hell-hole speak,*

for I knew you once. We lived in the same city, went to the same school.
I looked at his bloated face cut by the rain and said: *I don't think so –*
unless the inferno has so disfigured you. He answered:

My name is Ciacco, the name on every tongue, the entrepeneur
on every show, who made a bundle on the stock exchange,
owned five homes, invested well, dined at the gourmet clubs, who –

I heard no more for the spouting water submerged his monotone.
Poor rich Ciacco. I wept for him, my childhood friend,
the go-getting epitome of our epoch, until the plague winds came.

And then I felt my guide's hand upon my shoulder. It relayed the grace
Of a wisdom we had never known. I heard him say: *Too much pity*
confounds the soul. You have cried enough. Now we must leave this place.

IN THE FIFTH CIRCLE

Then my Master said: *It's past midnight.*
The stars are setting that first were rising when we met.
There's no time for dawdling

or turning round. We raced quickly to the other side.
Above us a spring broiled and frothed;
the water blank as lead

gave no gleam back. The sullen path fell steep
and hazardous.We followed the stream
down to the mist-blurred marsh

some name the Styx. There we saw men mired in mud.
LIke urban louts tanked up
in the backstreets

of our towns they mawled each other, head-butted, kicked,
snarled, bit. Some screamed out, lifting
their tattoed arms in rage

or pain, only to drive into the fray again. For some time
my master watched without a word,
then turning to me said:

You observe those so overwhelmed by hate
they damn themselves. Their lives
one staccato rant,

a bent mantra of 'no' and 'fuck you'; and what you see
is their black frenzy.
But underneath this water are those

who retired to the suburbs, yet their insipid lives
were warped by the same denial.
See how their breath repressed so long

comes boiling to the surface: a never-ending swill.
Do not go near. However parched, you must not drink it.
So we inched our way, my Master becoming silent –

and as for me? I begged God for greater insight,
the play and plunge of water
that mirrors light.

IN THE SEVENTH CIRCLE

In 2005 Dorothy Stang, a missionary nun, was murdered in Brazil for her work defending
the Amazonian Rain Forests

And so we reached the wood where all the tracks ran out.
I couldn't name the trees;
they looked like blackthorns bent against the Downs,

knotted together by the wind. Their ragged leaves hung limp
and diseased. And all the time
creatures swarmed above with dark wings, clawed feet,

grotesque faces. These freaks I recognized at once: the Furies,
who grasp the future pulsing in the instant
and shriek their warnings. Their high-pitched calls chilled

and slowed my blood. Then my Master said: *Before we take*
another step you must understand
one thing. We have entered the seventh circle –

it stretches as far as the burning sand. What you will witness
is so perverse, it tests and strains
the instrument of language, as a poet I should know.

Then a tidal wave of groans thundered in my ears,
yet I could see no-one. I felt confused.
Were the damned souls lurking in the tattered foliage?

My Master glanced at me. *Snap off a bough*, he said,
And you will see. I did
as I was told. At once, the severed branch began to bleed.

Who plucked me? It cried. *I am a man who suffers pain like you.*
Have you no feeling? Shocking in its redness
the blood streaked down my hand. Then I heard these words:

I am the murderer of Dorothy Stang, Sister of Notre Dame,
Mad prophet of the Rain Forests.
Although she whined for mercy I shot her through the head

three times. That stopped her blather about the deep ecology
of tribes and trees... His voice
was drowned by a mob of Furies whose razor wings

now lacerated him.Like trespassers, we slipped away.
I looked back once.
As if a hurricane had driven through, not one leaf hung.

Shanta Acharya

DAY OF RECKONING

I knew it would arrive one day
possibly in the guise of just another day,
never entirely revealing its purpose or plan
nor suggesting what it was supposed to mean.
It was not a rendezvous you could prepare for.

Life was stronger than my Self, I acknowledge.
Not that this conveys any more about life's mystery.
Every thing I valued had been stripped away
by sudden manoeuvres; love, poetry, freedom
I had treasured as sunlight or a breath of fresh air.

Whatever I had grown accustomed to expect
was perpetually beyond mine to have or cherish.
These exquisite toys were loaned to me for moments only,
to be renounced at no notice as if that was a gift.
Granted that change is the only permanent state.

But what is the bottomline to this act of creation ?
Sisyphus-like, I am cursed to futile labour,
eternally swapping toys for some promised nirvana.
Having discarded all my transient toys, I await alone
the coming of my day of reckoning. Preparedness is all.

Learning to live, amid uncertainties, with grace and faith;
even an element of charity. Doubting, but not sceptical.
Possessing, yet prepared to relinquish all,
if need be, in the right spirit; no remorse, no loss.
Not presuming, nor damning, I pretend not to prepare at all.

THE WISHING TREE

Children conspiring around the ancient
trunk of tree encircle it with their voices
clamouring to cover branches with tinsel –
calligraphically scripted dreams,
poems of love, coins at the bottom of a well,
prayer flags at monasteries
                along foothills of Himalayas.

A father hoists his son on his shoulders
tall as he leans to tie a prayer on a wing;
mother and daughter, hands outstretched
            cast dreams that spell the light:

If only I could walk
            in the hearts of my enemies…
Let father be able to speak again…
            Let my sister regain her sight…
Let mother come home soon from hospital…
            Let my brother who left home a year ago return…
Let there be peace in our world…
            Let no child die of hunger or pain…
May God hold us always
            in the palm of his hand…

NOT ONE OF THE MYTHS

Not one of the myths we make
will outlast the muting of our breath.

What comes and goes in silence
represents time's landscape of self.

So long estranged from my self,
I have created an illusion –

Carefully camouflaged
to welcome our re-entrance.

It is like passing from the object
to its unredeemable shadow,

Like leaping off the canvas of a painting
into the gallery of free spectators

Only to dread that moment of return
to another image that would recapture us.

A plastic version of all that passed among us
or others who unknowingly resembled us.

The imageless wind is the appropriate conception,
projecting the naked self, the final relation.

There arrives a time when the fiction is a mirror
image of itself; a thing final in itself.

Unable to discern between illusion and creation,
we have stopped revolving in self-abnegation.

After the wind has gathered its unique composure
and we breathe deeply the pure, fulfilling air

Our halcyon gestures resurrect words from silence
like conjurors revelling in tricks and games.

The myths dissolve in the silence that guts
our ineffectual, self-mutilating words.

Roselle Angwin

LET IT BE ENOUGH SOME MORNINGS

High tide, a wild morning, wild and stormy,
and you take the leaf-deep stony path
above seal-grey waters
          where the geese are dragged
through the sodden air like ripped-away prayer flags
in a crazy disordered dance, and the waves
slap hard on the mudflats' flanks,

and for once questions like
what use is poetry, if you're starving, or a refugee
squeezed between torture and war, or bleeding alone
in some dark alley
have momentarily flown, though left you unguarded;

but bent low over the creek the damson tree
drops unremarked a cargo of fruit
on the waters –

mornings like this
grey and green with straggled leaves
and the rain storming the opaque sky

let it be enough now to hear this one curlew keen,
to have one last bedraggled swallow skim the thick air
over your head, see the inkcaps' effortless
overnight arrival,
          to winess one small flower –
samphire, or a late marsh marigold –
struggling through black mud on its journey upwards

against gravity, pointing the way –
let each day be a small triumph, let it be
two fingers to death.

OUT OF ALBION

We called it Avalon, isle of apples
honey and eternal youth, this ripe breast
swelling out of the summer country's milky sea;
doorway to the paradise we thought would have no end,
beyond the ripples of all the pairs of opposites,
the tides of blood and bone.
                                        Flushed with our own
fullness, become accustomed to abundance,
we didn't see how easy it would be, how swift
the betraying journey through veiling mists

and the draining of the waters. And we
left upright, hard and angular, uncoupled
from fins and wings and creeping things,
balanced on legs that would walk us away
from each other, out into dry air
thick with its tumble of dead bees;

and it's only now, beached on stony ground
where our sureness falters and words stumble
after something barely perceived and already
left behind, irretrievable as childhood,
we notice at our feet the flood
of apples, brown glut amongst the burnt-off stubble,
shrivelled, ordinary as yesterday's platitudes,
so soon given over to the wet kiss of decay.

TAKING LIGHT

Only in the breaking
     of something
might we re-member wholeness
     the measure of it, its encompass.

The earth takes her light in a gulp
     of 2 kilos per second
and how we take ours
     is neat, in unpremeditated doses –

irradiated, for instance, by the faces
    of all who've loved us.
This is how the fragments
    hum back into wholeness.

It's unconditional. It continues. It's a fact.
    This has nothing to do with reason
And does not depend on belief.
    It continues. This is a fact. Remember light.

FEAR OF FALLING

after Pat Cox's painting

Night's long throat inhales the whole of you,
and Jonah-like you make the suffocating passage
through the darkness to the pumphouse of the heart,
then spark to flame, are swallowed
                 and combust, dispersed like ashes.

This is not the end but the beginning.
            You are not lost. You are reborn
nameless.

        Yes, and what you will remember
is not that sightless plummet into fear, the nothing
of it,
    but the christening of light, aurora borealis,
the way the body wears it, kaleidoscope
of all that you have been

and might yet be,
when the one who comes to love you
sees you as you are in all your frailty and glory.

Stand still and dare to let that lover find you.

           Be renamed.

William Ayot

ANYONE CAN SING

Anyone can sing. You just open your mouth
and give shape to a sound. Anyone can sing.
What is harder, is to proclaim the soul,
to initiate a wild and necessary deepening:
to give the voice broad, sonorous wings
of solitude, grief, and celebration,
to fill the body with the echoes of voices
lost long ago to bravery, and silence,
to prise the reluctant heart wide open,
to witness defeat, to suffer contempt,
to shrink, lose face, go down in ignominy,
to retreat to the last dark hiding-place
where the tattered remnants of your pride
still gather themselves around your nakedness,
to know these rags as your only protection
and yet still open – to face the possibility
that your innermost core may hold nothing at all,
and to sing from that – to fill the void
with every hurt, every harm, every hard-won joy
that staves off death yet honours its coming,
to sing both full and utterly empty,
alone and conjoined, exiled and at home,
to sing what people feel most keenly
yet never acknowledge until you sing it.
Anyone can sing. Yes. Anyone can sing.

CHILD OF THE SOUTH

For Pia Isabella on the Occasion of her Naming,
A Reponse to Coleridge's Frost at Midnight (1798).

The midnight sky is a deep, clear indigo
And the north east wind has dropped to a hush.
Outside, the air is sharpening, and a frost

Shines quietly to the quiet moon.
Across the water, two hundred years ago,
The poet of curses was stilled on such a night,
And blessed his beautiful, sleeping child.
Invoking wild nature and the God of what is
To mould its young spirit and to make it ask,
The rough romantic sat in wonderment,
Holding his child in tenderness and awe.

I have no child
And to me the frost speaks of cold not beauty.
No gentle breathing by my side
Can thaw my heart with paternal warmth.
And yet I think of you, far to the South,
New-born and something of a stranger to me.
What can I hope or dream for you
In a time of insatiable greed and selfishness?
I am not equipped to protect you from the world,
Nor to make its cruelties easier to bear.
I have not found the answer to loneliness,
Nor a way through the maze, nor the key to life.
I am what I am, a frail man
Who comes from a place of spiritual poverty:
A man who has tried, and usually failed,
A man who has struggled to give his word.

This then is my pledge,
My solemn oath, my one and only such undertaking.
I will not give you things for your appetites:
Nor gold, nor silver, nor tinkling trinkets;
Neither money nor power will you get from me.
But I will give you bluebells in the springtime
When the woods above Tintern are a lavender haze,
And the sweet scented chestnuts in their greening,
Are covered in candles like so many shrines.
I will give you slow, autumnal mornings,
Hunting for mushrooms in the misty fields,
And a mistle-thrush singing at winter sunset
His brave heart breaking on the twisted oak.
And he will give you the heron in his patience,
The kingfisher diving like a turquoise prayer;
A joy in being, and a taste for astonishment,
An eye for wonder, and an ear for God.

For truth to tell
I cannot shape you, nor would I choose to if I could.
So I'll spare you rules and give you stories
To keep you hopeful, imaginative and kind:
And poems and songs and chants and fables,
To help you to shudder and to shed a healthy tear.
For you will inherit a different world to me,
A world whose subtle forms and intricacies
My generation can scarcely imagine.
You will need cleverness, guile and wisdom,
And strength, and a star, and a willing heart.
All that takes thought and peace in the growing,
And the daily certainty of being loved.
The love, I am sure, you have aplenty,
Down there in the South where hearts are warm.
So I shall keep a place in the North, for you.
An old man waiting for a bright young soul.
There I shall polish my poems and my stories,
And sing back to the mistle-thrush as I wait.

IN FROM THE DARK

Barely housebroken, he comes to her
downcast but alert, offering her a stone,
a leaf or a feather that he hopes might show
the wonder that he feels and needs to share.
Every tiny gift, each incremental gesture,
brings the timber-wolf closer to the fire.
Now trembling, now curious, now aching
for affection, he stalks the warmth and light.
Sidling in from the forest of experience,
mind alive to the first false move, tense
body listening for the dry snap of memory,
he circles slowly round the flames, shudders,
then lays his head upon her lap.
                              This is how
the wildness dies. This is how we come in.

DEAD POET

It's good to be dead, to have the leisure
to talk to someone who might want to listen;
to be a poet at last, I mean a real poet, dead
as a door-nail and so somehow more believable.
There's no denying it was tough for a while
wandering around with all those feelings in a culture
where feelings were increasingly unwelcome,
where ultimately they were seen as a kind of curse,
where even poets were afraid of words like soul
and pain and spirituality.
        So, it's good to be dead,
to have given up all claim to being Percy Perfect,
the man whose mind was a series of rooms,
graciously opened to an appreciative public;
good to have given up the fruitless quest
for an approval that led right back to the cradle;
good to be free of the body I was shackled to,
aching to be free, to be some body else.

Of course, being dead has its compensations;
lazing down the years on this yellowing page,
waiting for you to browse your way towards me,
to find me "accidentally" when we both know
there's really no such thing as an accident.
I feel like the Raven, just three books along,
who waited for the Hero on the road to his doom.
From here you look shiny, young and invulnerable.
Bend closer. Listen. I have something to tell you.

IMMORTAL

He tore round the corner
judging it to the millimetre:
full-on, busy, impatient, and young;
expensive hair-cut, well pressed suit,
blue shirt with just a hint of red in the tie.
I expected him to look clean through me
but he stopped, dead in his inside tracks

like a prince in a myth at a crossroads or a bridge,
when he meets the one-eyed, wizened dwarf.
We stood, each waiting for the other to speak,
strangers yet not unknown to each other.
It was as if he wanted a secret, and I had one to give.
The hunger in him was palpable; the hunger
of a man who needs some solitude, or a drink,
or a friend, or a damned good cry. We waited
as his hand gripped and re-gripped his briefcase,
knuckles whitening as he made a fist,
then relaxed, then made it again, more rigidly.
Finally I broke the spell, said, Can I help you?
No! he said and stepped around me. No!
and he briskly walked away.
I watched him go,
watched the suit diminish, and cursed myself
for a fool. I shouldn't have said the "H" word,
you see, shouldn't have offered him my help.
When I was like that, when I was immortal,
I couldn't have born a kindness.

A CHANGE OF CULTURE

Everything happens very quickly.
The job, the car, the friends, the dream,
all vanish overnight.
Suddenly you're going down the pipe,
a nobody with nothing,
and nothing to look forward to.

You become a social security number,
shuffling shoes in an endless queue,
a little bag of memories, spilled out
in vain across a pawnbroker's mat,
sifted, sorted, priced and rejected.
You learn to lie – they expect you to.

One of us becomes one of them,
a transparent man with an arrogant step,
a jaunty smile and a haunted look,

the type you used to follow like a sniper,
picking them off with distant pity.
You learn to hate – selectively.

And then one evening, by the river,
your pockets stuffed with final demands,
you look at the skyline and see a sunset
so finely washed you catch your breath.
Sensing a delicate change in the seasons
you savour the world, and you are opened.

You wander home, trembling and amazed,
exhalting in a sudden awareness.
You kiss your wife as if for the first time
and later that night you wait up,
watching over her. When the tears come
at last, they feel wholesome and clean.

Sebastian Barker

UNTITLED

There is no place in which I have not been.
Deep in the doom of death I die alone.
I am the place in which all places meet.

I am the ghost in the living dead machine.
I am the clear white light in the dying bone.
I've sat and chatted with the rich élite.

Before the rocks were molten I was there.
I am the summer in a woman's eye.
Vast as the sea I am the unwept tear.

There is no forest, there is no desert air,
There is no bed, in which I do not die.
I am the cloisters in which the monks appear.

There is no place in which I have not been.
I've sat and chatted with the rich élite.
I am the ghost in the living dead machine.
I am the place in which all places meet.

THE FLUTING TRUMPETEER

Upon the very drop of night
        death, nor being is.
It is spectacular to see
        the mental consequences.

There is no follow-up to truth,
        death in the engine lies.
Don't give me resurrection, give me
        the truth of my demise.

No more, no longer, death has come
>   to whom it'd never left.
Nor am I circumscribed by this,
>   nor in truth bereft.

I am the sum of all I am
>   breathing God's good cheer,
Happy to be alive, to be
>   his fluting trumpeteer.

Matthew Barton

GENESIS

Here blinded with an Eye; and there
Deaf with the drumming of an Ear.
A Soul hung up, as 'twere, in Chains
Of Nerves, and Arteries, and Veins
Andrew Marvell, from 'A Dialogue Between the Soul and the Body' (1652)

A whole world in the wings,
weightless dispersed in dark
solution of the universe.

But I'm creating light:
slowly I dawn on myself.
Things take shape. I draw

strands from the ocean, braid them to
a finer pulse. Ages pass.
My Palaeozoic has begun to bud

its limb-fronds, leaf-hands. Everything I am
pours into me. I start to put down roots
of organs: spleen, brain, heart

spring and sprout. In delicate tilth
I plant eyes. I look
at all this from without –

must I tether myself to this
shrunk Eden? Is it too late to dissolve
back into wholeness? Must I pour myself

entirely into opaque earthenware,
cool and harden, lose translucency?
Now I see the seams of bones

begin to link up in a cage
to capture breath, to sunder me
from vanishing stars. But I can't stop

the flow I've started, the tug and pull
of gravity: I spiral into the rose
of the fontanelles.

And now I see nothing, nothing.
Just hear the double thump
of arrival and imprisonment. But know

I chose this, wanted this. I'll go through with this.

FORMS OF CARBON

I blow hard on the coals;
they answer with a fervent
river of sparks, flower up
flamboyantly, warm me back.

Is this what *I love you* means?

Not just a waste of breath,
a motion fanning each other's heart
into bloom, lit feast of eyes,
soft thunder of tongues?

Or something more. The slow
depositing of seams, compressing
sediment into substance – first
fuel and then finally
clearest, hardest constancy.

SKYLARK

Shuttlecock trembling on
the pinpoint of vision, spool
air spills itself through.
Little juggler holding
my head up, diabolo,
my heart stopped, spinning
the wind and plucking
a chatter of comb's teeth, clicking
your tiny Xhosa; bubbling, pouring out
pea-whistle arias as scales
fall from my ears.

(From the ground even bracken lifts
its prehistoric cochlea to hear.)

Does your tongue's needle
just quiver on territory, the pole
of fury and possession? No, sweeter: strung
through the tug of eggs to earth's
vessel whose skysail you are.

MILLENNIAL

August: choruses of sheep –
gargling bass and tremulous tenor
of senators blathering on about

an empire it's too late to save.
Broken polyphony in which each
complains at cross-purposes to each, not seeing

we're all barbarians now. The grass
doesn't have strategies, it's just bent
and nudges open cracks in well –

laid plans while the imperial idea
of order's being blown adrift
by raiding bands of rain and mist.

Yesterday was summer, the stretching
catapult of heat fired off
its final cuckoo, now has gone

slack and sodden. Out of sight
spores of fungus swell and stick
their thieving fingers in the pie
to get what's going. Time to render
whatever you can to whoever's still left –
Caesar, god, or the sycophant flies

performing their ministries, genuflecting at
sheep-dung altars, spreading the word
that everything's up for grabs; and after all

matter is what really matters.

Claudine Whiting Bloomfield

THE SONGBIRDS

We are all wounded,
of course we are.
Were it not so
we would all fly
heavenwards,
a fantastic fluttering,
and burn up
in a glorious blaze.

But something leadens our wings
and makes us adjust
and dip
away from the glorious sun…
an unexpected current,
a bent feather,
forgotten scar tissue.

And each morning,
despite ourselves
we rise again…
finding a current,
creating a current,
to take us skywards.

And each day we hear
horseshoes clattering on the road
worn a little more
and echoing less
then new again and humming
tin-sharp and quick in the air.

And each day the wind
plays her instruments differently
as the trees grow higher

and the branches bend
a new arc towards the earth.

And so I say,
as you preen your feathers
so straight and perfect,
it is the bent one
that keeps us here
where the symphony is playing.

FOR MATT

If I could see you again
I'd tell you
how you touched me
and I'd take you
to the green where they laid your flowers
where the sky opens endlessly
breathing a sway into the lilies
and roses that name
the love we felt for you
and your way
and your youth
and the unfairness of us losing you, but more
of you losing this morning.

And I wonder
what to do with the money I owe you
shall I buy a shirt and name it you
and wear it sometimes, but I wear you always
and so
so does the village
and all the buildings and all
the Sundays looming before me that mark your death.

And I wish I could hold you in the thinness you became
I wish you could have grown thinner still and so
still be with me
by the fire this Autumn coming –

you were coming to me to heal you, you told me –
and I'd wrap you in jumpers so thick you would feel
substantial to yourself, and we
would lay together in the light between us
eating oranges into the darkening
and you'd be the friend you said I needed

but if your moment came
we would peal
the layers from our bodies
and you'd grow so thin
you would slip inside me
and I would carry you there forever.

BETWEEN

friend
meet me   here
between the fields
and the garden gate
this fenceless, unowned
patch of wild.

but friend
come quietly
for the air
in me is still …
and needs
no stir of words
loosely tethered to the truth.

tread gently, friend
in this forgotten country
for my soul
rests
in this place.

Peter Brennan

SCORPIO

"I stumbled when I saw."

1

It hangs and tenses,
curling, flexing – through smooth and

deepening patinas
                    of eyeless
                                        ness
– (wierd) arachnid (weird)

twitching awake in a fog of waiting,

stitching together darkness that
                                        grips the globe
preparatory:

            the monsters
sweat and scratch are
dragged through granite
bloated limbs and glaucous
eyes   by inches – belching,
roaring

            blubbering now on the slow brown ground
scraping the stones, perspiring
                                        tears

in the sunthaw / filtering acids
                    to purge the wild

unseasoned seedbed of the year's harrowing

2

sa-shay – sway &

swivel lilt

& rise!

      lightning of dark
eyes fixing a wave's
unfurling

clack and click of the nimble,
supple mani-
pulating casta
nets

     smoothed along
            an endless poise of
                    thigh –

hither – the furnace – final

alchemy

VENUS AGAIN

She sits serene
above the loft
conversions opposite

moving unflustered down the weeks
at an unvarying
height.

Not to be mistaken
for an aircraft or a
satellite.

Herself
in truth
but calling forth

no tribute from the street
where her unblinking light
declines

the self
referring night. Her fragrant
lips encompassing

the fullness of desire – as we
in dream of ending
abdicate.

Her eye
unflinching
offers end-

lessness. Watching the mate
who watches close the
all he'd make his own –

dares him to warm
his heart at her cool pale
fire, her cloudy throne.

Richard Burns

THE WIND'S PATHS

The wind's paths
can't be written.
Neither ink nor blood

will code the wind.
Here is my home
inside the wind

and where I belong
in the wind's core.
Don't ask for me

in fields or houses,
on streets or mountains
or among companions.

Thanks to the wind
nothing I am
is usable. Indeed, I

am so changed by
the wind, soon I'll have
become invisible.

from BOOK WITH NO BACK COVER

I WILL SPEAK

I will speak. Yes I will. I will not, cannot be silenced. I am
     responsible for this seed landed here called Human

To root it through and through me till every pore breathes. That
     it break this sheen on the stuff of things.

That it scratch this varnished light a little. To trace
    what lies beneath it. That what be called gross or foul

Be charged with clearer breath. For blood, sweat, salt are
    particles of radiance. And shall be known by their true
    names

And for what they really are. But how perfection leaks from
    cracks in the bowl of now. And how time

Drips constant through the porous jar of presence. And how
    you and may waste, trying to fit shards together.

Yet I will speak. I must. And of these things too. This plant that
    grows from our speech in joy here I name: Community.

MOSAIC

We walked around the hill brow, and stumbled upon a
    temple. Tucked into a rock-fold and perched on its own
    outcrop on the far side of the valley. Down we stumbled,
    then climbed narrow steps, and paused,

Muscles aching, panting before its portals. It seemed half-
    built or a part-abandoned ruin. The sky tumbled in,
    etching clean-edged shadows. Dwarfed by lion-topped
    pillars in the broad, half-roofed arena,

Squatted an old man, white-bearded, barefoot, wearing no
    more than a loincloth. Poised on the patterned floor, like
    a lizard under the sun, statuesque in the late afternoon
    silence, self-absorbed as a child,

With mallet and chisel he played, and pegs and a line of
    hemp. And surrounded by piles of stone-chips,
    painstakingly he sorted – the blue and the green and the
    red, the opaque and semi-transparent,

The rainbow and spotted and speckled, the glossy and the
     polished, the rough edged and the pitted, the sparkling
     and iridescent, and the dull, that glowed, concave, as if
     swallowing light,

And those that held echoes or promises, gleaming or
     resplendent. And those that held depths, like eyes. Or
     mirrored skies, like wells. And those textured like
     parchment. Or tree-bark. Or flesh. Or leaves.

And my companion approached. And I followed and stood
     behind her, a little off to her right. And she asked the old
     master, *When will this mosaic be finished?* And he took,
     from a pouch at his waist,

An alabaster egg. And gestured to her to kneel, next to him,
     on his right. And closed her two hands over it, and closed
     his own over hers. And answered a single word, *Never.*

from THE MANAGER

THE AEON LIES TORN IN PIECES

The aeon lies torn in pieces but you shall mend it with
     me. With the slow patience of mothers. Who patch one
     threadbare garment

As a gift for a village child. Who may or may not be born.
     Who may not live at all. And, from such a Christmas
     as this, may even not survive.

What else is there to do? Play the Stock Exchange? Now I
     pay off my debts before I abandon money to the ghosts
     around the corner

Who, flushed in desirable residences at the smarter end
     of town, crease themselves in sneers at whatever does
     not fit them. Their one problem is

Life can never fit them. They fold and unfold their days.
   Invest them and insure them. But how long ago did
   they abandon longing.

On the corner, the little prostitutes have just stopped
   playing Hopscotch. Evening, and for them, time to get
   down to work.

Oh my sweet Sheba and my more than royal Jonathan,
   the history of humanity hasn't even started. *Da da,
   stari moj. Sigurno biće bolje.*

Jer dobro ti znaš, sve je moguće. It is a patchwork quilt,
   being stitched together in beauty. A coat of many
   colours. Life, my veil of splendour.

from CROFT WOODS

Is this the way for sure? I cannot know
But trust and follow one direction, down,
Deepening through darkness. There, may another light,
Agleam, then brightening like a shooting star
Shattered on ruffled waters of pale lake
Through this worlds clouded margins, break and shine.

Though rainbows, ribboned evenings, arrowed twilights
And orchestras of summer afternoons
In greeny plaited mazes wreathe light hours
And blind me to that ever-other kingdom,
Still may these voices wake me, interwoven
Through trees and shrubs, with scents of herbs and flowers.

As for the birds that wheel among upon these trees
Surrounding me, and call to their companions,
They'll be my questioned questioners, not masters.
My frank inquisitors, and testers of my spirit.
We shall migrate like them, on beating air,
And suddenly be no longer anywhere.

What love I bear you, world, I cannot vow
To promises, allurements, wedding rings
Of human projects cast in mere futurities.
If love is to be filled it must be now
By trusting in the heights *and* depths of things.
Love cannot grow, die, be reborn. *It is.*

Mirrors of music: see how here I go
Down, inward, through impenetrable shells
Of silences, through silence, into silence.
Towers of Babel, walls of Jericho
Tumble to petalled trumpets, pollen bells
Of flowers strung on unfathomable wells.

Spectres of blossoms, cloudy petal fluff
And wind-tossed seeds thrown feathered from their husks
Play melodies that cant be tracked on air.
Chords brushed from nothing, plaited lacy stuff,
Chains out of nowhere, cables combed from void,
Join death to us across their bridge of hair.

Conundrums of falling leaves, brushed honey-gold,
Cyclamen, autumn crocus, moss and mould,
Print coded passwords on my lips that yet
Are steeped and webbed in dew, still freshly wet.
These voices call from zones where dews have dried
And guiding hope and love rest purified.

from NOTNESS: SONNETS

SOUL OF MY SOUL

Soul of my soul, my soul's inner retreat
and nucleus, you still innermost space
that occupy no space yet light her face
in glance of recognition when we meet –
you, instant commonplace on way or street
as stone but quite untouchable in place

being her possessionless pure grace
and miracle – here, gone – too bittersweet
for being instantaneous, lacking name,
beginningless, unpassing, without end –
movement through leaves, sensed radiance and sheen
in all things, yet yourself always unseen –
in me be present yet and through me send
breath, spirit, ghost and extasy of flame.

David Caddy

ALCHEMY

Where the name of death is re-enactment,
dark flickerings may show themselves

or simply disappear. Echoes are answering
echoes in this terminus. Overheard conversations.

Space is being occupied by the thing-in-itself,
momentary affirmations waiting to flourish.

Boundaries between time and spirit recede.
Messages along this ancient path shout

or peter out. Time chops like an axe.
Joy in this, sensing something close

and that we are touching. Hands singing.
I am looking at the moon, into the fire.

I am looking where time lies down
into the body of another.

Anne Cluysenaar

from BATU-ANGAS

"I had now reached the furthest point in this direction that I had wished to attain."
— Alfred Russel Wallace, *Travels on the Amazon.*

This is the turning-point
    "where the streams divide".

He arrives at night
    through virgin forest, crossing
        invisible courses, the drop
            unknown beneath him.

On the day he gets to Javita
    the winter season begins.
        Early. It's February.
At home, spring is preparing.
    Here, the waters rise,
        There are fish in the branches.

He plans to stay forty days.

He knows that the white man,
    the 'rational', catching
        butterflies, beetles –
folding away onto paper
    grey ghosts of the fish
        he will eat for his supper –
only makes sense (if
    ever) in a different world.

By the time light fades,
    his hands barely hold the pencil,
        red and swollen from sandflies.
He soaks them in cold water.
    Iambic pentameter drifts,

phrases forming, unforming,
in place of good conversation.

Night after night
rain falls. The poem reaches
into his mind. The fear
of ignoble motives. The hope
of earning his own respect.

Must the joys of intellect
go with "the complicated villanies
of man called civilised",
"intense mental agonies",
"the long death-struggle
for the means to live",
while humans, here, go naked,
"bright and smooth", untrammelled
by "longing after gold"?

Temptations to stay for life...

That "distant dear-loved home"...

Putting down his pen,
he prepares two cups of salt.
Tomorrow's bargain-stuff.

from WATER TO BREATHE

I REMEMBER THIS MUCH

I remember this much: the sun
twisting in knots of cloud
down the glacial cwm, one field
then another lit up like reflections
in running water, as if

somewhere behind my back
a world bent down to look

at itself in ours and vanished
into all this – trees, houses,
black-and-white cows grazing –

and whatever I was had become
awareness only.
                            I came to
from this to my usual weight,
the scent of grass, a sea-gull
crying its way inland.

Since then, I'm a wave pulled back
from the sea, separated, delighting
in the eye of light at its centre,
the breaking of spume, but willing
to topple whenever into the tide.

THERE WERE DARK LEAVES SPREAD OUT

There were dark leaves spread out
so that the air between shone
as it narrowed, stretched, shivered.

A bird, never catching its breath,
sang invisibly, not hidden
yet not to be seen by me,

and from the gravel by my foot
a darker-than-red, a crimson
poppy swayed on a thin stalk.

It seemed we were all – tree
and air and bird and poppy and
gravel even – composing together

a secret no one of us
could know, not one escape.
Which breathes itself in us.

Lisa Dart

THE WORD

(John 1-1)

Once upon a time –

              The Word

Not aromatic lily.   Not spectre dove.

Not angelic light.   Not scourged flesh.

              The Word.

Not redemptive love.   Not white crucifixion.

Not deified blood.   Not bright raiment.

              The Word.

In the beginning –

Nascent.   Guttural.   Incandescent.

HELD

Not by nails hard into wood.
Not as a vinegar sponge souring lips.
Not in memories we don't have, but imagine we do:

shadow shrouding a cool room, a window's small light,
unrisen bread, a simple pitcher, red stain of spilt wine:
blood through a cloth's white,
                  and you remarking,
                      casually,
                          you'd come back for good.

Owen Davis

THERE'S NOTHING WRONG WITH A MAGICIAN WHO FAILS: A POEM FOR TRAVELLERS

'I moved on to the ground of light' - Asa Benveniste

Just to leave where you live,
Though you love it,
Is to invite a puff of pantomime smoke,
Smoke, and veils of corrosive regret.

Because your sojourn will be
Brief here as mine, there's
Plain magic in all you look at.
And the fine skein of despair,
To make laughter that bit truer.

Some of what you see will be
Invisible, or most of it. Ask Paul.
So tears mean even more,
The silver birch comes into leaf.
Gather yourself, and then go.

If it isn't springtime, so what.
Every season has skins it sheds.
A life it moves from, another it embraces.
Every season can shine.
To leave whom you love is an honour
Even the poorest of the dead can match.

That silver-topped cane by the door,
So nicely curved at the handle?
Take it along with you
It's a wand, of course it is.
Any person set upon going away
Shouldn't be without one.

But wait a moment.
In case of argument,
Let me say this:
No traveller yet has reached
Even the first corner of goodbye.
And there's no last line to any poem.

BASHO'S OLD GREEN POND

A lot of us know
You let a frog
Jump in.

You told the story well.
Famously, even.

But he's been jumping in,
To the benefit
Of your haiku.

For 400 years,
Give or take.

Don't you think you could
Let the poor creature
Do something else?

He'd be so eager,
By now, to jump
Back out,

I bet he could do it
In less than 17 syllables.

Let him try, Basho.
The time is right.

HOLY THINGS

1.

Holy things, sometimes
They're small and drear,
Their promises thinly kept.
The loneliness of God
I can believe in.
He makes much of dried sedges, doesn't He?
Of black pools and broken twigs.

There is stone in His face, for sure.
Today, there is.
His winter is a thorough lesson.
The poets who are left
Feed on what God hasn't got
The strength to let go of.

Clearly, the fish are angry in the rivers,
But how can they be helped, by you or I?
My grand-daughter looks at me
With dark reproach
For tearing off her shadow, so she says.

Blame must, of course, be borne
By someone, so here I am.
It's how I earn my keep,
How I know I'm loved.

2.
On this train, it feels like the rain
Will never be blue anymore
And the long clouds never shine.
A field of sugar-beet, a mile wide,
Dashes itself against memory,
Exactly like I pound myself
Against who I cannot help but be.
The stone, for me, is in my heart.
Today, it is.

Death is a memory, too,
That comes from up ahead.

It sails by the dirty window.
We're gathered up like motes,
Who sit here, papers on our laps,
Earlobes itching, listening
To the playful insect cries
Of mobile phones waking up
In the dark of our pockets.

3.
The eye misunderstands itself again.
And the soul, against all best advice,
Deals out a deadly hand of laughter.

Because of me, jet fuel scours heaven,
Penguins can't find their icebergs;
And weeping forests fall.
Your fault, I think, that a wave can reach
Cans of beans off a grocer's top shelf
On the far side of town.

And that's alright!
Because we set all this,
In measured verses,
Against the lovely snowdrop,
And the snowdrop wins.

We let it do that,
So God can feel okay,
So purple can possess the evening sky.

4.
I didn't want Death in this poem,
But February wouldn't listen.
I didn't want to think about
Something so cold.
I didn't want marble
Or the flailing hand of the mason.

The green of a living eye,
That's what I needed for you.
The turn of a secret smile.

A kiss yearning, between us, for itself,
Beginning when the sky falls down,
Making wide meadows of one small room.

But look at the clamorous piles
Of litter in the edges
Of the raining woods.
Dammit, look at February and the ditches.
At times like these,
When lines sigh as you write them,
I change into another person,
And the harm that dying does
Works inside me, free.

5.
It's Rimbaud's fault.
His fault we walk sometimes
In the wrong part of each other's heart,
And ourselves stand as crosses
Or lie as poor moss on the blind earth.

Tomorrow, I'd agree, has wings, yes.
And knows itself, at last, without lies.
Trains, as we guessed, avail themselves
Of platforms in the end.
The news is in: the hours have been
Travellers, too, coming our way
With lit faces, inventing us
A buttercup each, from scratch.

While the chiming stars disperse
The proper and urgent job of poets
Is to conspire against all but
Shy expectancy.
The rifle-butts are fiction.
The fuses, toys.

Over there, see, above the painted village?
The voice of God is a fluttering
Ribbon of light, overcoming
Even the powerful skylark.

David Donaldson

THIS ENGLAND...

This raft of rock, this precious fragment
Of welling magma, heaved out of equatorial seas
In utter anonymity in the world's youth;
This plug, wrenched out of Pluto's realm
To sear the atmosphere with fire
And buckle up to the heights
Of the Himalayas, Helvellyn, Snowdon;
This lava desert, this seat of fire
Heaving with the grind and guttural
Of slow tectonic quarrels, cooking
Beneath sulphur skies and for all that
Mere grist for the teeming oceans
In the slow-drifting deeps of time;
This limestone repository of warm primordial seas,
Coal-laden with the most un-English memories
Of steaming horsetail forests
And lumbering lizard horrors;
This Land-To-Be time and again folded, folded
Until wrapped once more in the cool winding sheet
Of the sea, receiving to its compacted core
The dying myriads settling on the ocean floor
Like steady rain; this buried image
Of What-Is-To-Be arising with the shuddering Alps,
Raising rough-cast shoulders of gleaming chalk
To a changed sky, its ancient furnaces
Belching fire; this heavenly hell displaying
Tolerant indications to suddenly familiar
Grasses, to the arisen birds and beasts;
This rumbling raft of life
Cooling, past its prime, scoured clear with ice,
Its pride of peaks vanished to strew the fertile plains,
Its fiery furnaces burnt out –
And alight in the bowels of long-toothed predators;
This crumpled cemetery of shell and bone
Embalmed in grave depths of sea and earth,

This island, cast adrift by the melting snows,
This wildwood of oak and birch, this wilderness
Of wolves and trackless wastes, marsh
And deep mirroring pools where curlew and bittern call;
This land of Men, of the chambered tomb,
The stone circle, the upland dead,
This far-flung outpost of imperial Rome,
This chaos of tribes flooding the land time
And again with bloody tides of plunder
And revenge. This chrysalis of an Order
Struggling to emerge: this Eden
Of drained swamps and razed wilderness,
Of rambling lanes and villages where brambles
And roses contend in the wild hedgerows;
This land of the commons, of lord and serf,
This property of the King, this province
Of the Pope, this realm of fervent knights
On holy quests and always, just a step behind,
The following shadows of plague and self.
This land of soaring arch and spire, of bricks
And iron ships, of steel rails, forged,
As by a hereditary twist, in the white heat
Of furnace fires; this land of satanic mills
And broadcast mechandise, of ancient sunlight
Harnassed to imperial sway; this drumming
Heart of Empire on which the sun
Has set; this hellish heaven of motorways
And shopping malls, fire-powered, fossil-fuelled,
Display of plenty, of awakened power; this store
Of legends and laboratories, this Realm
Of the Holy Grail, of the atom, split in two,
Of the Book of Life bound in a double helix
Discovered, opened up to view; this Realm
Of healing wells, of the Wounded King,
Of Avalon, of Arthur-Who-Will-Come-Again,
This Albion, Blake's Giant, stretched out still
Like the treeless hills, asleep,
                    asleep...

POEM AT THE TURN OF THE MILLENNIUM

Love is the Source. Love is the End.
Love calls us to awaken, for Love's sake;
To attend: an Age is closing,
Another dawns. Iron, Bronze and Stone
Have gone before. Now in their
Tempestuous wake, Mind
Like a migrating bird, before its wings
Are clipped or frozen stiff,
Must spread them wide
And seek the Summer of the Heart.
There, in the warming sun of a new dawn,
Open its eagle Eye to pierce the freezing fog
Clouding our perceptions' skies:
Their measured, flat, lawful-chaotic world,
Their obedient machines serving unmeasured ends,
Accelerating purposes, far beyond
The wrought world mastered in our Iron-Age dreams.
O, to awaken Mind in the Heart's rose
And see with new eyes what lies concealed
At our very feet! To strive to start
Is the Age's Dawn: to set foot
On the arduous climb from the old
To the new. From the splitting of the atom,
To the knowledge of the Heart.

Diana Durham

CRYSTAL BALL

Close up it is pure
white
dense
yet clear
all the way through
as the bulk of snow
drifts diminishes
to water

blue from space
or distance
sea-through
when examined
in a glass or phial

the transparency
of space
which is black.

When you fly
you see all the tiny houses
laid out
you think — how is it possible?

All the thousands and millions
of people
on the globe

they all have toothbrushes
and kitchen tables

they all have problems
and stories

in the crystal ball
of consciousness
often clouded and
always clear.

This is glob-al
the simultaneous
journeys of split
particles

it holds all
this is the magic of spheres.

Now that I have learned
to crystal gaze
I am not lonely anymore

I see only one
and everyone
and the Lord our God is one.

Glo-bal
the ball shines
it holds light
and sound
because crystal
contains a tone
a pulse
to set worlds spinning.

This is the fruit
that is not picked

the circles and stars
of spirals
arcing arms
flung out in space

for this is also dance
and I am no longer parted
from the tree.

FEED THE MOUNTAIN

There is a mountain
without form,
it is diamond
pyramid
city foursquare,
it is sun's gases
explosion of stars
silence of moons,
it is wisdom.

The mountain is alive in air
it is in fire
it is always there.
Feed the mountain
always first,
let its benevolence
shadow your days.

Let its shape grow clear
through the mist
order the root and ritual
of sleeping and waking
and gradually
the little abundant cycles
of your days will stitch
the larger, longed-for
patterns of your dreams:
and you will be able
to recognize them.

FATHER OF NIGHT

A presence is flowing towards me
out of the dark tonight

plentiful, endlessly
as endless as the road
that sweeps up to us

feeds itself
endlessly endlessly
under the car

this road is not beautiful
but it could also be
a way this radiance
pours itself out
into the night

the purple grey shades
of steel girdered bridges
neon-lit, white-lit
the giant bones
of overpasses
passing and repeating
sometimes the road
is faintly star-lit.

The black pours towards us
seamlessly
in branches and wide grey
stretches of flat river

the dark-rayed continuous
outpouring of its giant
movement steady
into the evening
that we are moving in now.

Simply like water
like black air
or the soft trajectories
of night rain
blown horizontal by the wind
or our rushing against
its silent wet softness

the presence of what we always dreamed
or never noticed
all the ways that we were always held
in this embrace.

Aidan Andrew Dun

from UNIVERSAL

CANTO V

Love with your mountains and punishing abysses,
transports and penalties, great heavy sorrows of the heart.
Love with your maytime joining of hands and early deaths of rejection.
Love teaching all hearts to break. And love rebuilding
under a blood-red sky the unloved with love.
Look! On the plane of cycling migratory lifetimes
where everything is volatile, unfixed and fluctuating,
you imply another, a second one, removed,
apart from the one who loves, toward whom you go
inching sadly across an ambivalent wilderness,
looking outside for completeness, old game of deuce.
Love! And you, self-denying true love soonest,
one day the sun of superconsciousness will dawn on you,
mind serene and cloudless in blue and gold weather,
mind beyond good and evil in the unified condition.

Week to week, under the transforming moon,
under the vivid constellations we crossed the hillside,
night-walking not far from the cabin at the timber-line,
considering the world and the separability of everything,
looking up into the floodlit heavens of Andromeda,
you and I in the North Indian night, most illustrious
spectacle of heavenly brightness these eyes have seen,
illuminated sky near the passes to Tibet.
Vast cosmos! Under a deluge of silver rays
I began to see the continuously brilliant possibility
of a night which is all stars, with multiple suns
for every world, insomniac paradise of fire.
And I remember once, discussing the mysteries
of that incandescent town-centre of our galaxy,
I found myself afterwards watching a city of embers
vibrating from a debris of pinecones dying down.
Then, while that symbolic radiance pulsated,

I chose from circling thoughts to question you,
(always planning another query in the darkness). And said:
Explain, Mahatma, prayers you say over the fire
when you seem to count rosaries down your finger-joints,
sixteen points from the knuckles to the finger-tips,
your thumb moving quickly in these computations.
And like the night-sky in the mountains you answered clearly:

There exists in you a never-ending deep need
to know what is hidden in my meditation practice.
It's good! I find a burning heart wonderful
when countrymen of mine in grey western suits
sleepwalk deathwards through automaton existence.
You drift east in the orange rags of a saddhu.
Steam-trains and bus-stations wear you down completely.
Dust-roads of Himachal eat up your determination.
But still you look out for the superconscious sun!
My flames reinforce prayer. Jai Shiva Shankar!
I am working inside the atom-planes with mantras,
trying to break the spells of duality holding
souls in the problematic pleasureful two-faced worlds.
Imagine! Limitless wheels of continuous birth
cycle all life-forms across the sensory realms,
form after form succeeding as carrier of life.
Spinning on in the way of the universe unrolling
the lower animals without individuality
revolve indefinitely by reflex or proclivity,
turning through births and deaths in good and evil.
Beautiful and strange is the hypnotising quality
found in far-flung worlds, with the mollusc in the sea,
the hummingbird visiting the red hibiscus flower
from where she drinks a nectar of the sun. Believe me!
I am sometimes surprised to remember the human face,
mind-winged in long meditations making my way
across other spheres, subjectivities and colourings of life.

Man in a less mechanical destiny
moves away from the automaton predicament,
from the unique vantage-point of mind, rare prominence,
surveying himself, crude freight-train of consciousness
hurrying smokily down the track of causation.
Now wheels turn with the actual sensation of turning.
Sparks fly in the hard work of hauling dead-weight,

ideas born from mind interacting with the body.
Now an individual begins to appear out of nature.
We see a black train that carries many people. Slowly,
one there starts to sense the grinding of the atoms
with every revolution of the huge creation-wheels,
seismic pain in the tiniest inexorable movement,
the agony beneath the calm face of every passenger,
the helpless situation of all trapped there in the carriage
hurtling down to the certain terminus of death.
This one mirrors the whole creation in himself,
feels even the condemnation of the stones underfoot.
This one changes destination in the station known as tantra!
For him is waiting the express-train called Shakti,
supercharged locomotive of the serpent-power!
In a vertical tunnel northward, in the spinal-column,
she rolls up faster through flashing lights, cobra,
huge red fires in her black hood hissing and blazing.
Through jewelled cities in the night, geometrical
flashing signs and hexagonal stars she thunders up,
breaking out from iron roads finally into sunlight,
apocalyptic sunlight beyond description or assessment,
light of the brilliant solar heart of the galaxy,
limitless light of the central sea of milk, blue and white
pacific ocean at the axis of tranquility.

Mahatma! Laughing, with a name of God on your lips,
you fell silent after your analysis of tantra.
I laughed also. And understood something.
Up in the intersection of the white mountains
I was becoming a follower of the transmission.
You were God's vagrant. I was dust on the road.
You passed by and stirred me into a whirlwind.
In blue air of the everglades I was spiralling upwards
carrying a cloud of white ashes on my forehead.
(I thought I was becoming a tranquil saddhu forever!).
And with more winged questions circling in consciousness,
(while mated doves rested in their rocking pine-houses,
slender green towers of mystical conjunction, trees marrying
heaven and earth with endless main-trunks rising),
I remained quiet in astronomical silences of night.

And our ship kept running for the Leeward Islands like a bird
that homes on magnetic lines and slow macrowaves

over the Atlantic, fastest winged creature of earth.
And out on the afterdeck, under equatorial stars,
I remember asking you, father, if other life travelled
out among different suns and planets of deep space.
And you told me then of those boiling volcanic holes
where somehow fire-eating dreadnought fishes exist.
And we sailed down through the Antilles, exotic
shorelines from which came seaborne aromas of spice,
clove and cinnamon carried on the sea-breeze at night.
And as we sailed on intoxicated with starlight,
little family of outward-crossing from the central hub
of old half-forgotten Europe, I heard strange fables,
myths of her life from my mother's own lips confessed,
as if she were freed from some vow of silence under way,
at liberty to speak in the passage through the sunlight.
And I was touched by her precious memories declared
as we sat there inclined in the white cambered prow.

I was carried back to a pale stretchered London,
haemorrhaged city of the blitz, all blood and sewage,
skylines of Hieronymous Bosch in scarlet and black,
the terrible stench of the erupting metropolis
mingled with the zombie mantra of Heinkel bombers.
(But God has given a new Teutonic generation
a fine love of everyone as a sign of forgiveness).
And I saw my father dragged from the balsa-wood belly
and fire-gutted fuselage of a night-fighter,
no more deathly navigating over Germany for him,
a great shard of Nazi steel in his neckbone, no hope
to shift or dislodge that ghastly implant of metal,
totally paralysed, all circular and sideways motion;
the neck, which acts like an intermediary bridge
between the two worlds of the body and the mind,
jammed with dense metal and unregenerate steel,
full of a living death-sentence of paralysis.

And my father Donald, descended from the Black Douglas,
lay in an airforce hospital-bed and remembered
the nights he courted my mother in wartime London,
she, ballerina, condemned to the meaninglessness
of mere entertainment, but making the best of it,
dancing in happy-go-lucky American vaudeville.
(From her womb unborn I speak one word ahead,

for already I fear our fascist western empire,
doomed to success, will dream in the end-time finally
a saccharine Yankee animation of the Calvary Road).
And my father Donald lay flat on a regulation mattress,
shot down from twelve-thousand foot by Eros and mortality,
heard many doctors pronounce him as good as dead.
And rather than condemn my mother to marriage with a shadow
shipped himself steerage back to West Indian shores,
a war-broken vestige of a man with no movement
inside the fiery hell at the back of his neck.

Outside of Kingston in Auntie's long veranda,
the invalid airman of thirty-odd, paralysed valiant,
lay week-in week-out supine on a bamboo shakedown,
ludicrous strains of Oklahoma intermingled
with the death-dealing scream of two Merlin engines
plunging by night through exploding airspace of Germany.
But a voice through anti-aircraft hell-fire spoke.
Someone. An uncle maybe. Donald, do you remember?
The place they call Doctor's Cove, m' boy. Doctor's Cove!
And he, the invalid, unable to kill the ridiculous
voice with a shake of the head, in such misery then,
turned as one terribly embittered man-unit to the wall,
for all his clear-minded longing unable to touch
his vision of Helena, faraway English girl.
But again through flak and cheerful American songs
next day the same obvious prophet spoke. And you
began to believe. And they carried you down to the sea!
And your slow salvation in the medical waterside began,
famous verge of ocean in colonial Jamaica,
well-spring that ran from the cliff-face into the surge.
And in the white mothering hands of the tide you lay
ten days till the tortured vertebrae unlocked!
And Aphrodite walked from the tropical surf erect,
high breakers curving in electric-blue to the coast.

HEART IN RUIN

after visiting Tintern Abbey

Heart in ruin, under the rain, roof gone,
your main structure half torn asunder, part-intact,
the wonder of you keeps a modern man sane.
Can someone explain how you came to rack,
fallen down from God's cathedral to a mere stone shack.
The paranoiac didn't care, he brought you here,
following chain-reactions of the Wars of the Roses.
Heart crowned with flames, beware, you need a Moses
to bring you from desert to restoration. Insane,
to lead the nation of Albion but not to know where.
Heart in ruin, have a care, remember these words
in the dark winter of declining civilization. Firebirds
are emotions, not clockwork atoms entwining.
Forget notions of the high-priest of science undermining.
Nothing lasts forever except love, the magenta.
In the trinity of head, heart and sex you are the centre.

The machine feels nothing but the heart lies open,
broken walls fallen in the driving rain.

Entering your space through the sign above your door,
interlocking circles of the common ground of grace,
heart in ruin, where has he seen your face before?
You're a woman, heart in ruin, who's lost her man,
the ace of diamonds in her hand vanished without trace.
Surely you're doing what you can to embrace the pain,
feelings still alive. You're not like the sinister brain,
that instrument of Faustus which makes this place,
a defunct world, of interest, a beach resort in Spain
where corpses sport in the sun of reason, commonplace.
You're the incomprehensible mid-season of God.
Ought not a sensible man caught in the mortal plot sort
what's cold from what's hot, reframe the shot, and start again?
Trees don't get bigger and bigger. They play a part in a game,
then fall like towers in the night. And yet, just the same,
all shall be surmounted with happiness like a flame.

The machine feels nothing but the heart lies open,
broken walls fallen in the driving rain.

Marion Fawlk

ALONENESS

Aloneness
Is a time of contemplation
The renewal of vows
Of containment in the sacred heart
It is not didactic
Or of intellectual persuasions
It is the living prayer of relationship
Of being with what is

Aloneness
Is not the anger of the wound
Or the warrior fires of Kali
It is the time of robing
And of the veil

It is the beauty of the bride
The ritual of marriage

It is the reverie
Of the holy spirit
The consummation of the blest

COMMITMENT

Commitment
Comes of itself
It evolves
It is not made

It is not a treatise of martyrdom
Or an act of bargaining exchange

Its power

Lies in the naked truth of feelings

Its refinement
Is lack of possession

It is a free land

And grows from its own liberated centre

Carolyn Finlay

THE RAIN AND THE CITY

Some of you become the rain.
Some become the city.

The rain falls.
The city stands.
Do this for three thousand years.

Those who have become the rain multiply themselves
into thousands, into fragmentary pieces
beating upon the stones of the city,
the walls of the city,
the blood-red roofs of the city.

The stones of the city stand as one.
It takes more than a few raindrops to crumble a city.

Those who have already fallen
clatter themselves into puddles, into runnels
in the cracked streets of the city.

Some of you tumble
through the gutters, the sluices,
into the river that coils through the city.

Some of you become the river.

The river sucks at the feet of the city.

The city begins to get fed up.
It chucks its worn and pitted stones
down into the river. Enough of these stones
will make a bridge, a dam. Dam the river.

Some of you become the dam.
More and more of you become the dam.

The dam grows so wide that it becomes
a major thoroughfare, with shops and cafes.

Some of you become the shops and cafes.
The shops and cafes become busy.
They throw their rubbish out of the window
into the river.

This goes on for two thousand years.
Some of you become the rubbish.
So much rubbish collects that the thoroughfare
widens to become a windy field.

Some of you become the field.
Some of you become the wind.

Beneath the field lie the stones.
Some of these stones are the knobbled bones of the earth.
Some are worn smooth by black subterranean streams.

Some of you become the knobbled bones.
Some of you become the black streams.

Some have been weathered throughout time
by rain, wind and hail.
Some have been cracked by ice.

Some of you become the smooth stones.
Some of you become the hail.
Some become the ice.

Those who have been the rain for five thousand years,
swap, and become the cracks in the stone.

Those who have been the field
become the rain.
The rain falls, greening the avenues of the city.

The city loosens its belt, belching
playing fields and boulevards onto the windy field.
Small local farms become petting zoos.

About a hundred of you become the pets,
with five of you taking the role of the angora goats,
and half a dozen the Vietnamese pot-bellied pigs.

The wind swoops from cold mountain peaks,
ruffling the soft fur of the goats,
the mink tippets of dictators' wives.

Some of you become the tippets.
Three of you become the wives.
Two hundred of you become their shoes.

Those of you who have been the wind
lie still. Those who have been the rocks,
roll until you find the black streams, and rest.
Those who are the shoes, dance

and continue dancing through the night,
through the red lights of the city, across the bridge, past
the playing fields and the farms, past the dam,

across the stony fields. When you reach the mountains,
slow down, and begin to climb. Those of you
who have been ice, rain and hail, become the river.

Those who are the shoes, keep climbing.
Do this for a thousand days, until the rain
begins to fall once more.

Two more rules.
All of you stop doing as you are told.
Do not begin the game again.

Rose Flint

CITY AT SAMHAIN

Rain wet, the pavements are slick, slippery
in these thin smooth shoes. Mist
clouds the lights into cloudy spheres
that float soft moons above us in the dark;
the city becomes gentle at this hour.

Yesterday the clocks rolled back
their big confusing loop of early night.
Only lovers have found a use for this
between time, day's finale in the dark.
Heads alight with raindrops,
fingers curled around each other's warmth
like rubbing sticks to make a fire,
they go slow twostep through the rainy town.

Alone below the cathedral's
glancing flights and swoops of floodlit stone
a busker spills his glittering music
in a gift of gold across the empty square;
his saxophone laments the human heart,
all separations.
The gliding lovers coo his songs
beneath their breath: prayer, mantra, promise.

On their way into a wilder sky than this
the Spirits pause, wait quietly, taking the form
of statue's shadow or sinuous grey cat
as they listen to the keening beneath
the worn out notes that spell *baby, forever.*

Hold me close, my lover, closer. Tonight
the dark between these paving stones of light
seems deep as space, as if we danced on glass.

THE SOURCE

They have taken the soft birds from under her breasts
cut the blue roots out of her veins.
They stood inconsequentially talking of meat and money
while they peeled away the skin of her arms
where the tongues of deer and bear were recorded.
They dusted their poisons into her spaces, let her bees
fall out in a firestorm. They cut back her hair
and singed her scalp so nothing will grow there now
no green horses, no lianas, no lizards, no babies.
They drank the water out of her eyes, dammed
the silver water table in concrete so she stares blankly

but the tears still come.

No one can quench the source of the river under the river
and myths and dreams and healing still flow out of it.
We know she lives. She is the voice of the newborn
and the Ancestor, the gaze of the last white tiger
and the flower that breaks through the road.
She is the red thread of life in all of us;
she is tomorrow and we cry for her: *Mother, free us.*

WEARING THE FOUR-QUARTERED SKIN OF THE ELEMENTS

As if a salamander shucked off its brilliance
or a phoenix, still glazed with albumen, birthed
through this saltwood fire, heat haze
ripples serpentine stones into water,
fusing four elements, making a fifth sacred thing
visible in shine: a spirit-skin, flexing,
stretching out its pinions, its plumage of gloss.

Do I know the spell that allows me to step out
of the sand that surrounds me
and walk into that place of intense heat
and transparency? Sand blows into my eyes
so I cry out blindly, but if I could slide

the four quartered skin of the elements
over myself like a membrane of light,
I'd become clear, meniscus of crystal,
far-sighted each way.

Fire would seal me into that spirit-skin,
hissing and steaming – it would feel like a coat
of rippled cellophane electric as liquid quartz.
Air would breathe me up into its global dervish,
Water would swallow me – I fish-silvered, mirrored,
drinking in wisdom under the ninth wave. Earth
would rock me, root me deep so I could learn
the web of the world's patterns and know
in my own body the distortions we've made
in the balanced fabric of things
as we stumble myopically in and out of life.

And I'd go where the elements go in their dreaming.
I'd follow migrations of weather and seasons,
ride the mirage and the ice, glide down the steep face
of a woman's tears into the cave of questions
where the world's answers sit in the four directions
patient as tourmaline, or the future
that's still not chosen. They are waiting
for someone to come seeking their saving grace;
they have all the time in the world, as we have.

Let me be brave enough to step into that place
of heat and transparency and be seen: caring,
wearing the world's living skin on my sleeve.

JOURNEY OVER BLOSSOMING STONES

River Wye 1979

Near the outset, in the first fiery summer
we made the journey over unfamiliar maps
stones in our shoes and flowers
budding under our skin, our tongues closing together
over the names that spelled that early season

kingcup, birdsfoot trefoil, Aaron's rod, monkey flower
yellow petals tumbling like kisses or confetti
and we were stumbling over a dry gold plain
– white sun and miles of light blinding the distance –
and found the great river's primal spring
in a thin vivid upwelling, spilled sudden crystal
divining the fertile winding
through ochre and granite and grassland to ocean.

      The water so small in my hands.
      Your hands over mine
      and your clear certainty:
that this was the source, the beginning, this
diamond flowing that ran through our fingers
becoming the river, shaping our lives,
holding us in its flood, sweeping us
into its days, its broad years, its beauty.

Cora Greenhill

SPICE OF AFTERLIFE

If my immortal self would have me speak
it would be with the freshness of these Christmas roses
words cleanly abrasive as rosemary
understated and full of promise as those clematis buds.

And the sense of the words would perfume your thoughts
as lovage flavours soup
would spike your dreams like fennel.

When the words flew overhead
you would feel the wind in the sails of your day.

If my immortal soul would have me write
the poetry would be like a herb garden:
hardy, healing, and well-harvested.

DEVOTIONS

Atmaram is preparing
something called Puja.
Adam is making tea.
Atmaram lights crumbs of scented substances
in small brass bowls,
intoning softly
ringing bells.

Adam stirs and dunks the bag again
considering the strength
before adding just the right amount
of full cream milk.

Atmaran wears an elegant light tunic
moves with quiet precision
minimally
calmly whisks open a black umbrella
before stepping lightly, incongruously
yet entirely congruent
into a wet Welsh westerly.

Adam, crumple waterproofed
and wellingtoned
steers the mugs on a zigzag muddy journey
of husbandry, seeing to this and that.
Sacrificing his mountain-striding
forest-fearless strength
to carry the cup
his gift of homage
and serve it to Irena.

Atmaran will call us all to prayer
with bells
and I give thanks
for ordinary acts of care
humility and grace.

THE STRENGTH OF CUPS

1. Full cup

I am the deep-cupped bloom,
called dranculus, dragon arum
or, commonly, stinkhorn.

I rise waist-high in Crete's May heat
open a crimson throat as long as your arm
to hold you in my wine-dark centre

my sparkling sailor of the wine-dark seas
my man behind the mast
my mast, my thick stamen

I draw you into where there is no space
only the strength of desire to be filled:
(a strength I find no name for
in my Thesaurus)
that seals us both hermetically to pleasure –
Hermes and Aphrodite
                              become one flame.

2. Minoan cup

The strength I find no name for
in my Thesaurus
I see was celebrated here
in the sacral knot
the spiralled pot
the snakes that slither and glide
the octopus that clasps and sucks

where the throat of the crocus,
the mouth of the cave,
are invitations to enter
the labyrinth's path
be drawn in
sweet body of the dark
to source the scent...

of a woman stood taut-waisted
breath drawn up, chest filled with fire,
bare breasts flared:
holder of power
holding
golden serpents
arched from her arms
arched upwards
poised: the power of poise
not pounce
it is the power of holding
not the strike
not the strength of the sword
held high, but of cups

hand-molded
of baked earth
strong with the heat of the sun
and great bellied jugs
strong bellied
breasted
strong bodied
beaked
the body thus strong
supports the voice
the voice rises
gives song to the stars
and all is held
in a strong web
a strong fine web
finely designed
hand made
divine.

David H. W. Grubb

WALKING TO GOD

"1 cannot walk an inch
without trying to walk to God. "
    Anne Sexton (1928-1974)

You get past childhood and yet
returning is a constant calling.
You get to the words and yet
they say so many different things.
You get to the garden and see your mother
and your father there and cannot decipher their smiles.
You get to see yourself in a small room of toys,
dreams, games and bowed-down prayers.
You get to the room of constant light and know
that there are others here, all light, all silent.
You get to the centre of the light and know that
there is the being of light and that there are no edges
and that everything you realised before is not real.
You get past yourself and your memory and your story
and everything that has been meaning and let this light
clothe you entirely; its radiance; its knowledge.
You know that at this moment you are with God.

EASTER STORY

And if there were no Easter, what then?
An ancient tale waiting for its time,
perhaps later some other child born
to die attended by lepers and miracles and
a cross that bleeds for two thousand years.
If all they saw had been ghosts then the glorious
tapestry of lies breeds a rainbow of
perversions, a panoply of visions stitched

by poverty, politics and survival strategies,
a history of conviction catching on its
own crude credo, the beauty of bigotry.
So we have poetry without truth, gestures
and inclinations. The plot was botched
from Bethlehem through to a green hill
where words were nailed to bone and it was
only a man who dangled brilliantly on
a cross of sham. And the world moved
on waiting for the next nutter, the tribal
desire for messiahs, anointing boys who
should have kept to carpentry and never have
listened to the one who was off his head.
Cock-crows and denials and later walking
with the dead to keep themselves alive.
Nothing else was possible.
They began to believe.

ALL OF THEIR FACES ARE BECOMING SUN

When they get out of Kosova there is no space for words
for words and their meanings have been stripped from them years ago
and only in the last running days has it been possible to have this conversation
in the centre of a forest
in the centre of a field
in the centre of a rainstorm
in the centre of the night darkness
in the centre of a pile of rubble
in the centre of a playground of glass
in the centre of burning stones.

When they get to Kiikes there are faces they begin to recognise
and for some of them faces they dare not recognise and for some
of them the faces of those who betrayed them and for some of them
there are the faces they would wish to simply ignore, not see
in the centre of the crowded tent
in the centre of the shower rooms
in the centre of the truck or bus

in the centre of the listing of names
in the centre of the circle of eyes
in the centre of the hands that greet.

And after the hours of the final journey when there are no more soldiers
and no more checkpoints and no more forms to fill in and no more
strangers in the midst in the centre in the journeying and no cries
of your name and no questions from other men and no children without eyes
and there is this drifting between sleep and movement
between what has become and what you once were
between the hidden words and using your name again
between a house on fire and a house of screams
between the death of animals and the stealing of light
between the people who gently repeat your real name
between the place of your dying and what you have now become.

AFTER THIS MIRACLE

After this miracle has taken place
one man races into the nearest pub and says "give me a double"
and the double appears.
Others shuffle off to ordinary things; they need the ordinary
to race through their veins in case they cannot regain control;
coffee, a glass of water, pottering about in the garden, a crossword
puzzle, kicking the cat will do.
Some, however, cannot let go. They need a church, a solemn bell,
odour of candles, silence of pews.
They need to look into the eyes of the crucified man.
They need a nest of prayers.
They need to know how to change.
Is that the sun? Will it snow? Will the children return to games?
Sound of rain. Clocks. Windows letting out and letting in.
Each day another reminder and another journey.

And what did we really expect?
When I see the priest shall I tell him or will he tell me
and what will we both be doing in these words and tellings,
about the actual event; and what shall we now call a miracle?

The sensation of rain and wind on the mind
and seeking for things to forgive
and the mystery of so many birds' nests this year.
When we look out at the moon we look across the world
and across the spaces and into the eye of God.
One miracle. One life.

All the bells of all the holy places now shed gold
and repeat "forgive, forgive, forgive!"
And between all the bells the new and future silences
are cast wherein there may become another miracle.

Geoffrey Godbert

THE BUTTERFLY

Lightly brushed, the butterfly's patterns of
silence and flowers are falling from their wings
as petals fall from rainbows; perhaps that
is why we reach out for them and try
to see through them to the sky we would
ascend to become cracks of colour on rock
faces, or the trunks of unclimbable trees.
All that remains on our finger-tips is
silk, a diaphanous bruise of dust,
while water-colours run from the clouds.
Like all colours, it is light of life
they seek and must find, sometimes in a day;
when we see them dully despair, we enfold
them gently in a handkerchief and wave
them airborne and floating like blossom.
That journey is as fragile as night-fall
on the earthbound monotone at our feet:
it must carry by breeze like a message;
and cling very still to bright sunshine
next day, if it is to bring the reply.

I AM AT CROSS-ROADS

I am
at cross-roads;
there is danger:

I have
imagined
everything.

IN THE OLD DAYS OF THE HEART

There is a barbarian I know
who still does not process his words;
unbelievably, he writes them
on bare paper with any pencil
which comes to hand, without a thought
for himself or posterity,
just like romantics used to do
in the old days of the heart.

It must be the same madman
who still lifts the phone to hear poems;
or, if there is silence, to speak them:
into the mouthpiece; to anyone,
including himself, who will listen.

REMEMBERING A LIFE-TIME

I am about to tell the truth
about my life and times and how

on one occasion I met
Cafavy with Rimbaud
in Alexandria:
                it's true;
if only you could ask them
they would say they remembered.

I remember their sing-song
of myths like real voices
and their fearful bird-calls posing
as love, pleasure, elopement.

I remember the new life of them,
faces that had taken a life-
time to become real faces.

I remember the new life of me
now as real as a life-time

of memories and their dreams
I always wished to remember

of truth, without destroying the myth,
its own legitimacy.

THE TRAVELLER

In memory of Howard Fry

I can tell you this, that when
he died the entirely expected
happened: flowers continued to bloom,
the sun to shine and the moon to rise
as if on a heavenly sigh
of the spirit of him waking
from what had been his silence.

What was totally unexpected
were the sharp breezes of his memory
rustling exotic labels
marking the travels of his life,
stirring his empty luggage
with the names of places he could
visit again at will; and one
he would see for the very first time.

Jill Haas

from THE LAST DAYS

I.
How many days of human eyes
scanning the horizon to search
and saw   and saw

not God;

How great a stock of crystal eyes
and fiery cars show skyward
gaze and probe, but find

not Word...
nor hint of a shining face or
wrath-filled face or *any* face.

How many eyes look down again?

Too long has something sat in the sky
by the Name
and names, and alias of God

But Not-god:
not even a glimmer
of That which over centuries and generations
was somehow made trivial and workable,
so easy to grasp

It was torn from every living thing and every rock
to re-emerge in human form
and man-sized.

II.
For too long you've mistaken a
duck-pond for the ocean,

believed the Old Man of a thousand
church ceilings or stone-carved Buddha
or Olympian King or gentle, many-faced Mother

to be more than an instant and atom
of Its image...

Such a god could only be unhearing
and far away and ever more brittle –

until you'd learn to live without it ;
until even the notion became odd
and finally, irrelevant.

(Not God, it is
           the heart that's vanished,
that was big enough to fill with
           a Presence as inward as the self
and yet creating all things :
           a Godhead that won't be squeezed
into a form or Name
           or rolled up in a heaven)

Assuming you choose to feel
that the image of a godless, and uninspired world
is suddenly outlandish;

that you undo, in turn, each
ribbon of the man-made pain
you've borne, and invariably blamed on heaven;

that now you understand
other faculties than mind

(assuming – you even care to use them.

then music from the strings that no one plucks
           becomes proof ;
and visions   and magic groves ;

And the yearned-for   most fabulous Treasure
is yours

by sinking into It
by flying up to It

now by running   now by dreaming –

by forsaking words   and a single direction

(or if not,   then at least

by the Power of Wanting.

                           I see,
a creature in an ancient desert –
itself millennia old

and for those millennia
unmoving   immutable;

kept alive by man-tears
and a regimen of blood.

But now
the old rains refuse to come

The thing scents an unknown liquid
– feels the desert flower   and throb beneath it;
at first   a gentle tickling
yet soon unendurable:

the creature begins to stir.

It is dew from
        The new-born era

Become mist now showers –
        A magnificent torrent
Pushing wide   pouring into the desert

(if instantly absorbed
        the life it inevitably bears
at least beginning.

Keith Hackwood

from 100 SONNETS OF GALACTIC LOVE

SONNET VIII

I remember your hand in the clear waters of the stream
Among the glimmering crimson pebbles of desire,
Tickling the rainbow belly of the
Salmon of Wisdom.

For years you crouched and stroked there
With your eyes enraptured, your ears suffused
By the murmuring wonder of life,
You stirred and breathed and cried.

And now, in scales more mesmerising
Fresher than the melting snow,
You swim in every river

Flashing passion through a prism
Like silver arrows brilliantly
Murdering my fear.

SONNET XV

Once again, Love, the green has swept me up
And multiplied my passion
In plateaus, escarpments and folded rills
Moving like souls down Hay Bluff.

A lark saluted my tread
In holy elegies to the Sun

Your fingers curled round my own
When the freedom began

And transmitted your gleam
Like anvil sparks, like
Energy in endless expanses of motion,

Or the horse on the hill silhouetted,
Knowing that Christ, at Capel-Y-Ffin,
Held all the aces of the raven.

SONNET XXXI

Angel, I have heard you sing from the stone
Fountain in the centre of my soul, turning my
Ears to light, such fluidity and grace. Here
I am, in service to the children of your song.

Pan came first, from the wide spaces on
The wild green branch of life, with wondrous
Isis shining indestructibly,
Hovering in a dream of burnished gold

To dance in circles, awash with
Smoke, hand in hand with rainbowed
Chiron, my masterful guide.

Yesterday I was lower
Than a blade of grass – Now
I see that healing is alive.

Stephen Hall

COLUMBUS RECURRING

— half your world is in neglect —

Dreams: dark matter of the psyche. Dark matter: unconsciousness of the cosmos.

Dark side of the moon: satellite-mapped. Dark side of the sun: as yet unrediscovered data-source, the eye of Horus.

Taxonomy of the subtle Earth: devas, elementals, and great Pan.

'We're life too': the underground masses who break down and free for use all that the green ones build.

Exquisitely stowed in logarithms: the other half of the universe, the half that's smaller than you. Man, mislabelled worm, how galactically great you are, to a quark.

History: the visible busyness of man paddling across the vast sacred quotidian of woman.

No upside-down in space so let our maps move, cartwheel: propose a horizontal Chile, and Africa on top.

Cabala, alchemy, Freemasonry: underground western streams, in neglected bogs that glitter curiously, and irrigating the grand gardens of pleasure and improvement named Shakespeare, Newton, Mozart.

The secret east: calculus, and clockwork – and printing, four centuries before Gutenberg.

The other life of George, the driver, unsuspected by the whole firm, by all but those who enter the shrine of his spare room.

The life let go for your sake, of the woman who sleeps by your side: elsewhere her inner sister takes it up.

Of Americas, no end in sight.

FIELD THEORY

Imagination is the invisible all-encompassing master field, and Poetry, its agitation.

All other fields are contractions of this master field, manifesting only for as long as they can resist their native freedom in the Imagination.

Present science floats entire and precarious in a field of sober low-dimensional prose.

Seen aslant, this primal field is a teeming sea of seed-syllables, proto-poems, micro-haiku – each threatening, if sounded, to unfurl a world about you, the parasol of a lyric with egg-delicate sky, or to spool out Mahabharata-size, acres of canvas, circus-crazy, trailing translations, movies and dedicated websites.

Try this experiment. Relax and let all lesser fields dissolve. Take a sheaf of learned papers, schooled and impeccable – and tip them like factory fish into their great original alphabet soup of Imagination. Observe their rigid linearity ripple and twist. Observe them relax into the greater space, forswearing A4, sprouting feathery fins and whiskery filaments of meaning, leaping and contradicting. Imagine their sense go nonsense, go nursery rhyme, go lullaby, ghost story, exploding absurdist joke, go finally beat scripture – hoarse whispered or pavement-scrawled revelation, church of this moment only, to be washed away in the next shower with the dog-ends and fast food wrappers...

In this field the force is felt as an irresistible invitation to play.

SCHOOL FOR LOVE

Leaning between worlds, neither yards nor light
years distant, a great prince scans the High Street noon,
its blaze of August, swooping invisibly
among the shoppers, workers – where to moor
his magnificence for a further human sojourn?
A perfect, pubescent glowing girl sashays
across the zebra catwalk, at her ear
the latest jewel-box mobile, as a tanned

and tattooed ankle swivels above jade toe-nails –
not her, not like her this time – too transparent.
That hulking blur behind her on the kerb —
shift focus on wheelchair and carer, and what it bears –
between the red-raw features shaving-nicked
and huge, clownlike, cheap outmoded trainers,
long fingers grip the armrests, as of a throne.
Yes, him – go deep, it must go deeper,
pierce this reluctant brethren, penetrate.

The window fades, the prince draws back and quietly,
gravely, weighs whether he has the strength for this –
a sixty year station in prospect. He previews
the thousand casual insults, barefaced blankings
of neglect, sadistic intimacies
and tastes the long monotony of evenings
as fashions mutate and governments revolve,
when showered, toileted, pyjama'd, he'd be parked
before the TV's perpetual banal outflow
while bored young nurses, fidgeting their phones,
shaped entertainment of a livelier kind.

Neither moments nor decades later, you pause
now on your island while traffic throbs,
and on the pavement opposite a wheelchair waits.
The great muzzle lolling in the sunken chest
jerks suddenly up, swings in a great slow arc –
unblinking takes in the pigeons busy
with trodden crisps, the tiny flowering moss
above the shop sign, the cashpoint queue, and pans
to you – leonine amber blinks once, locks in.
And as the traffic's soundtrack fades, and framed
within a slow green corridor that seems
to tumble, siting you within its range,
a tawny lord's great head now turns

and sniffing you, begins to rise and plunge.

GOLD

A vein of living gold runs under my days –
not a day passes but it outcrops and splashes,
slapping, tickling me into remembrance:
wherever goes my road is holy ground –
and up ahead I hear Naropa lives
who tossed his disciple Marpa's homage of fool's
gold dust to the wind, crying
'don't you realize *everything* is gold for me?'

Alyson Hallett

THE STORM TRILOGY

(Written in Ronald Duncan's Hut, Welcombe, North Devon)

1 – Cycle

The world is still as death;
the sea's glass lens shooting back
the sky's dull veil
       wheat fields frozen upright – each blade
pacified by the wind's wild flight:
      I do not know where it went
  do not know where anything goes in that moment
before the storm

      the spill hovering before the wick.

  When dark clouds break
         they spill their bellies
      into parched earth: each drop bending dirt
to mud, scripting the path's new texture
      before lightning snaps the land's last trace.

        Rain rummies on the hut's wooden roof
  hidden streams form across
      the land. I sense them there:
new fingers rolling over rocks, tasting clover
        scooping the grip from beneath a sheep's foot.
  New streams, newly cleaned ferns, new buds seizing
the replenished root –
      the damp summer scene scented
     as a dream just woken from –
      as if loss might possess a perfume of its own
released in the second after one thing dies
      but before the next is born.

Out here in the borderlands
        edges are too clear: the cliff the sea:
    the sea the sky: even Devon and Cornwall split
    on the valley's ridge. Each breath,
        each whisper is a bridge
    and I am living lowly, staying close to the ground
                        for even the slightest tremor
        can cause havoc.

This is where the elements breathe;
        I've been here before, lived on an island
    that was less land than shore.
    I've known a man canoe out to sea
        and never come back
    I've seen a man fall by a hotel door
    and die of a heart attack. Death, the potential
    for death, given space in the place
        where hospitals and roads are so far
    away the words "come quickly" mean hours
                not minutes:
        and there is a taste to these places –
        metal and honeysuckle – sweet and raw
        the blade's edge so present as to almost be
                visible.

These borderlands are where I live –
        life elsewhere is not life
    but a giving away of something essential.

                Each night now the Plough
    bridles the plot above my house
    the sky's scythe slowly reaping.
        I welcome its sickle, the gourd
    of its belly, the belligerence of its posture:
    where there is live-stock there has to be dead-stock
            a farmer once told me
                    tossing away a breathless lamb.
    No room then for sentiment, no pause for pity,
        life's strings laid almost too bare to bear.
    But not quite.

Two nights ago I took my grief to the crying gate
        to catch the sun's last shining.

There, instead of despair, I found my feet
pinned to earth as though pierced
        by a pitch-fork's prongs: truth
took hold and span me round –
I gripped the gate for balance
         pressed to the outer limits
        of my own fragile intelligence
and suddenly the sun was rising instead of sinking
        scooping my siblings on the other side of the world into light
        their night falling into my day, first stars
barnacling the same unflinching sky –

This is why, in the borderlands,
          out here on too many edges
  even dying plays its ring of sound
      without impediment
            dropping its reddened head
into a pool of water
      like a baby's brow at the old Saxon font.

2 – In Obscurity

Inside the fallen cloud crows fly low
        yesterday's twinned cormorants
nowhere to be seen.
The sea stretches for a mile or so
combing the jutting rock with metronomic surf.

Waves rise inside the body of themselves
        like bread before baked and broken.

No light comes shining through
      and yet it is not dark: Obscurity is the place
  between the two;
      the shadow of the shadowland
  the border drawn without line
 a vagueling space no word or conscious thought
might define.

Everything is abandoned –
        your hair turns to weed
                your body to sand and stone
and you dissolve like the good dog who went out one day
        and forgot his way home.
    Not danger exactly; more bitter than that
more sanguine or simply hopeless.

They will not launch the Life Boat – my flares
        are too damp to be fired or the flare
disappears without trace in the fallen cloud or,
      most likely, I do not bother to let the flare off in the
               first place.
    In moments such as this you want to
know if the unknowable thing fits,
          try it on for size,
              stumble through the mirrorless hall
              towards you don't know what.

The wheatfield is still again,
feathered ears of corn conspiring with salt-tinged mist
      to make a dream;
    if you were to slip into sleep
    you might mistake neverland
for a place more real than this.

            Madness, madness, madness – obscurity snatches
  every sane thing and sends it dripping
through the mangle.
  A snail cowers beneath a thistle's leaf
three black-horned sheep crowd a corner
    the sea stands upright as a seal at a circus
            freed from its horizontal leash.

      Madness, madness
      and the thought, for a moment, of stepping over the
cliff for surely that nothing, that fine particled cloud,
      must be capable of holding something up?

And then the storm returns.
    The rumbling sky
      cracks of lightning
        and not an hour passed

since the last fierce onslaught.
                              In Obscurity, the candle's wick
          hungering for the spill
                    and the bright task
                         of burning its own body.

3 – Host

The wheat moves today
          offering its burnished antennae to the wind.
  There is no hint of a dream:
          clean edges abound
                    even the cows are black and white clean
          keen at the fence to meet a stranger.

I keep checking the sky
for a sign or a hint:
                              but no: no rain, no crackling
          clouds, just wheat swimming in wind beneath a bright blue sky.

          A small bird bleeps from the ground
          flies to the middle of the golden swell
  and disappears between growing ears.
                    I snap a thistle's down between
my fingers
          greet a dragonfly
            follow a butterfly to the stile.

The sky's sill is back –
today's horizon a neat blue line
          demarcating sea and sky –
  I'd like to plant red geraniums on that distant ledge
pepper the predictable curve with gashes of crimson.

I do not trust its unflinching presence –
                    the horizon has been sucked dry
          of its usual measure
                    and all I can say is that today there are
          lines where yesterday there were none.
Even the valleys have opened,

clefts of land dipping between two treedoms
rivers running through their cores.
              Way beyond, the flicker of a
wind turbine blackens the sky with three canonical wings.

Many blues, a host of blues,
              small blue flowers, big blue waves, the clear day
                      rehearsing the scheme of itself
              regaining semblance
after the whip of wind and bladed wave.

Is it more beautiful this way?
              They will sell more ice-creams today,
                  rent more deck-chairs at Westward Ho!
              but more beautiful? I cannot say.

Perhaps it is my curse to prefer the short view
              with an imagined length
    a storm rumbling from the sky
as gods whip horses to speed their chariots by:
              they fit together, I know they do, fit like a foot
              inside a shoe –
    cloudy one day, clear the next
alternate weathers clamouring for expression.

  But
I cannot help miss the rack of clouds
              the disturbed view, the drenching
as I pound the path towards this remote hut:

perhaps only those who need to be broken –
              poet, corn, seed –
await the darkening clouds
unable to bear loveliness too long
              before missing the storm's wilder song.

Adam Horovitz

VESSELS

My god's an empty vessel that I fill
with all the flowers from my small garden;
ragwort, cyclamen and tulip, daisies,

even the bindweed that chokes the roses.
And they of course take pride of place amongst
the fruits; the redcurrants, gooseberries, pears

and greengages. I work in this garden
full with love, although I've had to learn it,
and at my side my cats frisk the long grass

for butterflies, slow-worms and frightened birds
lost in the bewilderment of first flight.
Am I their god, do you suppose, that they

bring me dead offerings as if in tithe:
emaciated, inedible voles,
their quizzical snouts slicked with day-old blood,

spiders broken beneath claw-loaded pads?
Am I an empty vessel they must fill?
Out working in the vibrant summer sun,

the only essences of truth I've found
are nestled deep in almost everything
beneath traitorous, disillusioned skin.

Even my two thuggish cats, sauntering,
skilled in murder, contain these purring sparks.
Manipulation's mankind's skill – only

we make vessels to suit our purposes.
What better way is there to begin than
in a garden, where tender, partisan
hands can raise up the heads of crippled plants,

where – mouth pursed in imitation of the
morning sun – a lip's brush opens roses?

My cats, in their limber, instinctive state
understand this, as their offerings show.
Remove these two and all equations fail.

They give no gifts because of who I am,
they honour the garden with their patrol,
thanking me only for what I've begun –

this green cup awash with the spores of life.

A VOICE IN THE WOODS

Last week I found a voice
in some wild corner of the wood
singing unknown melodies
and throwing itself into the mouths of cows.

It followed me home,
zipping from bluebell to fox to gravestone
        giving each a different song
When the door was shut
it warbled its way in through the letterbox.

I caught it, laid it
on the kitchen table,
sliced it open with a vegetable knife
and let the cool wetness of it
stain my skin.

 Inside, it was translucent –
a cow's heart
   made of fading lace
   and half-blown dandelion clocks.
 I left its wisping corpse
under the cooker,

hoping to seed
   the house with song.

Libby Houston

GOLD

Going this way, the swell of the pale clay
tilts cab and shuddering machinery
at the woods coming up over the brow from the east
beaded with ilex and shaggier sycamore,
and dark as fur.

And in the hour before sunset,
that low hour of gold,
his plough turns up gold.

He stops anyway, it's the time
he likes to enjoy his unentailed treasure.
God never made this field or held
the wood in place any more than he cut
diamonds.

– But I'll give him the sky.

He jumps down, rolls a fag, sees a rabbit
bounce off across the track, a pheasant
parting the skirts of the far hedge; these two coins.

When your dreams tire, they go underground
and out of kindness that's where they stay.

Battles of tens were fought round here,
battles of hundreds, battles of ones and twos.
That gold was battleworn before it left the mint.

I don't want it, he said.

And as for you – what, a dozen centuries
less or more – and whatever fellows of bone and sherd
kept you company,

why should you be poked awake
and made to run through it again
and again, and again?

All the facts, all the possible
crowds of them I can imagine like
pressing up against the railings of fame
for a name, I tell you they're
bars when you're on the other side,
a fool can see that,
say that –
say anything.

I'm not headed to be slashed out of this by a sword
but I've as hard and full a story as any of yours.
The morning frost's as cold.

If you're gold, you can wait.

He laughs, flicking the butt into the furrow with them,
climbing back up to rattle the wind's teeth,
go gouging earth again.

Must be something like twenty years ago
I dreamed I turned up a hoard of gold
ploughing – that was where I woke up.

A LITTLE TREACHERY

From this turn in the path, look –
that web of twigs is the last,
the last skin if you like.
Beyond that, the sky's bare.
Whatever. Don't be afraid.

When we step into the full light,
all your woodland skills then suddenly
useless as fishes' gills for air,

the worst thing is regret – don't let it in,
don't give it ground enough
for a fly's egg.

All this, these, clotted stacks of leaves,
ramson aroma, the colourless flowers you love,
hairgrass like fountains, saturated mould,
steep cries, dry wings, fern plumes, the nightingale,
green tripwires, freckles of light, rot-muffled falls,
this blinkered scope, soft, sharp, partitioned, still –
feast on the old familiar, imprint if you want, now.
We don't come back. You know that – and the stories,
no looking back.

We say good-bye to it once just.
Then. Not yet. Once, at the edge, where
what's beyond – no one's said more than that.
Except – and I'm sure it's true –
nothing to fear. Except, to start at least,
we walk arms wide, palms open.

So, the cargo you've picked up, the significant cones,
the eggshells, mousebone, beakbone, flowers, stones,
leave. There, at the edge. Like an offering
at the gate. You're shivering.

Don't be afraid.
I can go first if you like into the bright space.

I shall be walking backwards reading your face.

Alan Jackson

DEAD MAN'S CREEK

Oh I hid my head from the mighty wind,
Yes, I hid my head from the mighty wind.
But the wind didn't mind, no, it came right in:
No, the wind didn't mind, it came right in.

And I ran away up Dead Man's Creek,
Yes, I ran away up Dead Man's Creek,
And what did I hear, but a dead man speak?
Yes, that's what I heard, I heard a dead man speak.

And this is what he said, said Welcome, friend;
Yes, that's what he said, said Welcome, friend.
You can stop off runnin' 'cause you've reached the end,
You can stop off runnin' 'cause you've reached the end.

But I didn't believe him, and I jumped for shelter,
No, I didn't believe him and I jumped for shelter.
And the place I jumped to, was a helter-skelter,
Yes, the place I jumped to, was a helter-skelter.

Round and down and round and down
Down and down and around and round
Till I hit with a thud in the mud on the ground,
Yes, I hit with a thud in the mud on the ground.

And here I'm resting with a hundred more,
The lame and the weary and the sick and the sore.
Yes, here I'm resting with a hundred more,
The lame and the weary and the sick and the sore.

We don't do much, but we don't tell lies;
 No, we don't do much, but we don't tell lies.
When you go underground you lose the lids off your eyes,
Yes, when you go underground you lose the lids off your eyes.

So, welcome, welcome, welcome, friend.
Yes, welcome, welcome, welcome, friend.
Have no fear, we all meet here in the end,
Deep in the ground where you grow and mend.
Down with the dead men, you're welcome, friend;
So don't be afraid: we're going to meet, going to meet
going to meet   in   the End.

SALUTATIONS

I bring you salutations from the planets,
I bring you watch and welcome from the stars.
I come on embassy and with no weapons,
But with these gifts of words, ideas and symbols,
Traced from the stuff in which the high ones travel,
Transformed by medium and by distance,
By the ignorance of this small person,
Into shape-thoughts suitable for earth.

Through the barriers of death and dark
That are set about this dwelling place, I came.
Must please excuse the lateness of my speaking:
So fearful was the atmosphere I passed through,
So fierce the time and terrible my landing,
I was smashed out of the meaning of my visit;
And when murmurs of it slowly came to surface,
I'd been so shredded then compressed into a type,
I was staggered and disheartened by the chasm
Between what spoke within me and the day.

Then came my story like one of your long novels
Of which there is no need to speak here now.
I sum it up by saying: As I lay,
Listening to the message I had in me,
Repeating and rehearsing and comparing,
Alternately being weakened and made strong,
One came up very close and sat beside me,
Looked into my eyes and said: "I see you,
And even if only I, it is enough.

Don't hesitate and don't mistake your meaning.
You are what your in-thoughts tell you, that is sure.
Stand up, go out, speak to those who listen.
Your embassy begins at every dawn."

So my vehicle of travel was revived,
The robe of love and light that is my home.

I bring you salutations from the planets,
I bring you watch and welcome from the stars,
When I remember I remind you we are spirits
Who can wake from death to life and lose our scars.

The word is clear, it is: to abandon
The word is clear, it is: to suffer pain
The word is clear, it is: to surrender
The word is clear, it is: you are not lame.

I bring you salutations from the planets,
I bring you watch and welcome from the stars.
Be brave, all you who care for this endeavour,
We have yet to live and die through many wars.

Norman Jope

A PLACE THAT EXISTS IN WINTER

for Lynda

I write to you, of a place I don't inhabit,
a place you inhabit in my imagining.
I write to you, in an ink pressed from silence,
of a place addressed by your absence.
I write to you in the shadow of snow
and it whitens the words I write.

This place exists in winter.
It's a city in which exterior forms
are drab and matt and hunkered down
as if a tarpaulin had been draped on them all.
There are grey skies and a layer of frost
on twigs and thorns, and as you lock the gate
a thin film of ice is disturbed
and rusted railings creak.
Drizzle freezes in the air as it falls
as you wait for the suburban train,
tuned in, against your will, to the howling of dogs.

Here, the undersides of leaves
left un-disposed of in the streets are white
and ghost roads lead past fishbone trees
in frost-whitened dawn, to nowhere.
You wait and think of the dead shells of crickets
that, three months earlier, filled the air with their bowing.

Someone has brought a bike on board,
encrusted with snow as if carved from ice.
As snow begins to swirl through the vents,
magazines and books are dusted white.
Towards the centre, commuters stand
and their coats smell dank and ovine.

They are twice their summer size,
leave slushy footprints like the menses of dreams.

You cross the subway with the crowd,
past buskers and spread-out cloths,
women wearily holding out dresses.
On the Metro, there are more dark coats
with an odour of damp and soot –
ill-smelling men in baseball caps
blowing into blackened hands,
students buried in textbooks,
matrons lost in translated thrillers,
mothers consoling babies,
indomitable crones in headscarves,
old men in trilbies, a frightened woman
with apocalypse in her eyes –
gangster plankton, Krishna devotees,
all heading to streets and malls.
It's a different world down there,
half bus, half air-raid shelter
and escape's on a dawdling escalator
as a woman strips to skimpy panties
on a series of posters, more naked as you rise.

There's a thin brown sludge on the pavements
like fudge, or lentil soup in a can left open –
drifting snow in streets, across graffiti tunnels,
leaving moth-scale patterns on coats.
In the silvery milky beige-grey light,
a black dog's as dark as a lump of coal
and the castle, seen from the bridge,
is a sculpture of whalebone or nacre –
doorways are cleared with spindly brooms
and the dispossessed are busy shovelling.

Breath stiffens as it leaves the gap
between hat and scarf, in hesitant light –
then, once more, the snow begins to fall
and anoints you as you walk
from client to client, dispensing your language,
carrying your textbooks, wearied by motion
and the split-shifts you despise.
Your lush blonde hair hangs over your shoulders

and, from the faraway Atlantic,
you're the subject of a Gulf Stream of lust –
but life is short and the reach between us is long.
In a place that exists in winter, sooty buildings rise
with rusting balconies and broken neon
and, when clouds clear from the curve of the moor
and the Sound begins to shine, I think of you
and check the weather where you are. But now,
there's no forecast I can check –
in a place that exists in winter,
you make a living dragging your bones
from one conversation to another,
a discoloured pulp of slush on your boots.

So I offer you a respite.
In the white confines of the mall you enter
for a well-earned hot chocolate, Santa Claus appears
in the guise of a blonde in shiny black boots,
her sun-lounge-golden thighs exposed
beneath her carmine cloak, and instead
of the usual flier for T-Mobile or Nokia,
hands you an envelope, beneath
the wreaths, moons, and violet stars
the Christmas decorations here amount to.
She winks as she does so and you think
of the mischievous things you've done,
have not quite done and would possibly do.
She presses herself against you
for a moment, then she's off into the crowd
of housewives, mall brats, over-excited peasants,
down the escalator, under the glued-on stags
and other remnants of the Ice Age.
You lick whipped cream from the glass
and open the package. Remove four pictures.
Each has a sponsor, a website, a slogan
on the back, but that's misleading.
Wait, and I'll tell you what you see.

The atrium, five storeys of it, reaches into the air
and the sky is draped on the roof like a sheet.
Inside, the light's extreme and artificial
and the weather's peripheral and mute.
Outside, the dealers are shivering,

blowing their hands, so obvious
about their illicit business that you smile.
A two-minute walk across the tram lines
leads you back to the Metro
with the envelope stashed in your bag.

Hour gives way to hour on the civic clocks
and you tick off your appointments –
meeting teachers, junior executives,
students, millionaires and engineers
in brown-upholstered rooms.
Correcting grammar, spinning out stories,
dancing between your language and theirs,
shaking hands and pocketing florins.
Night arrives, with its clatter of shadows
and slush hardens, cars scrape past,
the city settles to its screens.
Again, you enter the Metro,
minding where you sit, jealous of your space,
nursing your shoulder and your leached-out voice.
Again, you walk through the subway
to a plaint of pentatonic scales.
Again, you turn the key in a rusted lock
and the dogs of the sixteenth district howl.

Four pictures, considered in your room.
The first is of a black sun, rising over a swamp.
The second, of a man and woman bathing in milk.
The third, of a queen who plants her coins in rich warm soil.
The fourth, of a starry lion, crimson-white against a purple sky.
Your attention shifts from the city to these pictures,
delicately tinted, antique as they are.
You picture Mercurius – a red-clad woman,
handing out brochures in the mall –
you imagine yourself licked open
by a lion made of stars, on a vertical journey
and this wintry place becomes the theatre
of spring to come, of transformations
this city, like all others, can bear.
And I write to you, from the maritime West,
the departure point for so many ships,
of you, in winter, staring at these shapes
and dreaming yourself in ruby and gold.

Outside, the fog creeps over snow
and, in seven hours, the slow green train
will clatter towards you, with its bleary load,
on its way to the lead-lined city
where all remains possible, if currently sealed
like the mammoth's tooth at the door of the mall –
but it's time to step from this winter, love,
and time to melt the ice from this poem
and step from the moraine its massed words make
as, outside, in the Devon dawn,
a blackbird sings, unflasking his voice
and our shared, stretched spring returns.

LUCIA OBSCURA

She walks on bare rock
across the island
with the darkness under her feet,
with the deep sky over her head.

She walks naked over the lava-field.
The camera craves her attention.
There is no wind to rustle her hair.

Why is she walking and in what direction?
The camera pans to a room in the city,
an empty space where she laid down to sleep.

No one can chart her movements and, in any case,
the film runs out. Who points the camera now
must do so cunningly, from love

of her, of the skin, of the promise of sun
in a landscape that is other, where distractions are not
and all there is conspires to perfect her walk,
that riposte of the living to the lies of the dead.

Georgina Yael Johnson

SANCTUARY

In the place we call home,
cool Carmel rock shelters
wounds of warriors and slaves,
staking refuge in nations;
new homes crafted on ruins,
draped with timeless shock,
as if, in leaving this place,
we forgot pieces of ourselves.

This is a mortal place –
a blaze of nature
and vengeful memory;
the scattered crumbs
of homes torn open.
Too easy to fathom
the normality of life,
tea and politeness;
the desert heart-beat of days.
Do the dead know borders?

Yearning through earth's etheric,
nature is a refuge to itself.
Here can we sense the
wind-bourne kiss that moved Elijah?
Yes. We too nursed vengeance,
Like you, sliced good and bad.
Like you, we find ourself
in this subtle garden –
pathetic and human.
Let's pass over.
Together, with melting flesh,
Cherubin of fear and mind
hoodwinked;
absorbing freedom

where beasts drink freely,
newly named;
blossom of almond trees,
incarnation of joy;
and man and wife
in seamless unity.
We are thistles, rock and sky,
moving waters christening sea breeze.
Purified by sun, we are dog
mindlessly charging space.
We are this hawk,
hovered in stillness,
a blue core of divinity –
playground of angels.

It seems so simple now.
No sacrifice, terror or rage,
no big bang of dreadful judgement,
no measure of pain,
will rampart Eden's gates.
Only soft, invisible longing
to blend with living;
love finer than changing worlds;
only peace in sweet ponds
timelessly waiting,
as the word "other" lacks momentum,
and we welcome ourselves
Home.

Only then, Eden comes to us,
Refuge, sanctuary and bliss.

BENEATH

Loved beyond beloving, beauty
rises in mists of prayer;
yearning the fullness in your becoming
free from treachery, despair,
yes, even free from me.
Let me fall beneath you, light,

caressing you out of yourself
that you might rise.

Releasing every cell and hair
and accent rejoicing mirror of form
to wider bliss and wiser still;
alive in unbecoming robes
so naked, let me wait...
taste breath of eternity
in ecstatic suspension
beside you, in Eden
until sun's coming golden signs
the way to earth.

MAGDELENA

                              did they dare it?
                        or did love burn so whitely
                    it cleansed need to manifest love
                as mortals – we hungering half-circles
                              yearning the whole
                                 yin and yang
                        two fish just grounded

            writhing apart two fish
          on mooreland as
        river flows onward
    unheeding, Magdelena loved freedom's
      currents, holy a priestess, unearthing
          sacred lust for living, so God
                gets laid on earth

Nora Leonard

WHITE SHELL WOMAN

Patiently I wait for her,
at the edge of twilight
where shadow is blue
and moonshine spills
across the water making me
foolish and drunk.

Night is her season,
and she sails along to meet me,
the woman adorned
with white shell and coral:
huddled on the sandbank
we converse about dreams.

When I was a child
her ivory skirt would come
billowing through my window;
shivering in awe in my
pink flannel sleeper,
I'd greet her at the sill.

For years she has
abided my defences,
ignoring my denials,
treasuring all the fossils,
the calcified tears
I now measure in bulk,

and when I most feared
the drowning of the spark,
I would pick up her talisman.
Listen, she whispers
from the conch's rosy oracle,
It's the changing of the tide.

Now, at the new moon,
we sit like conjoint twins,
women in waiting
for the hidden pregnant seed:
we'll nurture it in darkness
before offering it a birth.

I have lived to an age
she no longer looks old;
in the pulsing of my blood
I often feel her presence,
grief surfacing in waves,
and solace from grief.

An opalescent light
spills from my heart
into her basket.
It's a fathomless pool:
on a night like this
the moon's its reflection.

OPENINGS

A dim memory
wrinkled and frail,
shivering in the mind
like leaf-lace in winter.
The turn of your head:
an unexpected pang
both a shudder and a lure.

It was so long ago –
a place discovered
and quickly forgotten.
We've all been there,
the strange part of town,
the gape of an alley
where the hook of a dream
caught and drew us in.

You thought the night
would go on forever,
stoical to the end
until you stumbled
into the courtyard:
limpets of light
clinging to the brick,
a thousand ghostly whispers,
the flickering wings of gossamer moths.

For here they are:
here are the doors.

A lock intended to last forever
crumbles when the key is ready.
The heart hesitates,
fearful of the source;
beyond the threshold,
Good Friday, Easter and Christmas
are unfolding at a pace
hardly to be believed.

Opening will bring remembrance,
but do not fear the bones
tumbling from their confinement.
Some are dead beyond caring,
but there are others here
who deserve a second chance.

And you are their chance,
you are their opening.
What at first seems so alien
will become the familiar.
Hasten, rediscover the portal:
be generous with your courage,
embrace a new hope.

Grevel Lindop

TABLE DANCE

Forget the table, there isn't one. Nicole
likes American rock music, and un-
dresses in red, just the bra top,
wisp of lace for a skirt, and the G-string –
though the perspex stilettos might hint
at some fairy-tale beginning, glass slippers
of a Cinderella who stayed out far too long
after midnight and never went home.
Now she twirls on glittering toes, grasps
the pole as if to turn the world upside down
but it's herself she spins, and I'm amazed
at how high over me she can kick,
at how low she can bend and still look back
between her legs at me, that enigma,
those eyes unreadable. But when she comes close –
the podium dripping with discarded red –
it isn't those dark curves or the almost-splitting
fruit of her labia, nor even the poppy
burn of her mouth that I must watch. And no,
I won't always follow her hand down
to that teased nipple, or the gossamer preen of her
finger tracing sweet involutions of self-
love between her thighs. No, it's the eyes I go for:
beyond their diamond-burst that far darkness
where nothing's faked or has a price, where we
are both naked, and we know what we know.

SCATTERING THE ASHES

At last the rain cleared and we found a barley-field
where the crop was knee-high, and in our town shoes
paced the lumpy furrows along the edge

until our trousers were soaked. My brother held it out,
open, and I pushed my hand in. It was like
dark corn, or oatmeal, or both, the fine dust
surprisingly heavy as it sighed through the green
blades and hit the earth. And like the sower
in that nursery picture ('To bed with the lamb,
and up with the laverock') we strode on, flinging it
broadcast, left and right, out over the field.
And there was no doubt that things were all in their places,
the tumbled clouds moving back, light in the wheel-ruts
and puddles of the lane as we walked to the car;
and yes, there were larks scribbling their songs on the sky
as the air warmed up. We noticed small steps
by a pool in the stream where a boy might have played
and people fetched water once, and wild watercress
that streamed like green hair inside the ribbed gloss of the current.
And then I was swinging the wheel as we found our way
round the lane corners in a maze of tall hedges
patched with wild roses, under steep slopes of larch
and sycamore, glimpsing the red sandstone of castles
hidden high in the woods. And the grit under our nails
was the midpoint of a spectrum that ran from the pattern in our cells
to the memories of two children, and it was all right.

THE CYPRESS TREES

Waking at night, in darkness, I stepped out of bed,
knowing perfectly well where I was:
bare wall at an angle, door at the end,
tall shuttered window. And outside
the long garden with the cypress trees –
the moon-shadows, the gentle Italian night.

All wholly familiar; only my hand
struck a wall where no wall should have been.
I felt along it. The door was missing too.
Perplexed, not frightened, I still knew the place –
polished wood floor of the passage outside,
white plaster wall. Yet the door wasn't there,

the wall was in the wrong place. Then I remembered:
I was at home, in England, no longer in Rome,
where I'd slept last night. But far stranger than that,
though I touched my English wall, this room my mind
insisted I stood in was not in the Roman hotel –
the mirrors, the yellowy light from the via Margutta –

not at all. This was some unknown Italian room,
yet intimately familiar. I was lost –
laughed, almost, at the metaphysical comedy
of touching a room I was quite unable to picture
whilst mentally standing in one at a different angle,
in another country, unidentified

yet thoroughly known. At last, groping my way
to the actual door, I grasped a knob. And then
my room came clear in my head, as if a light
were suddenly switched on. Where had I been? –
awake, alert, amused, and somewhere else.

I'm patient enough. Perhaps I shall get back there.
Will it be with fear? Glad recognition?
Elusive, troubling sense of *déja vu*?
Enough that I remembered; or that the place,
for its own peculiar reasons, remembered me –
the slant wall, the high, shuttered window,
the unseen blue moonlight. The cypress trees.

GENIUS LOCI

Sometimes, as death came nearer, it seemed to him
that he would not mind becoming a genius loci,
a small protecting deity, for this place
of folded green, silver-grey rock, May blossom,
with its glimpses of stars, roots and mud.
It could be, after all, only a brief diversion:
in a few, or a few thousand or a few million
years it would be burned or covered with ice

or the planet itself, or the universe, would disintegrate
or otherwise unbe. In the meantime
he could tend it, discourage destruction, gently induce
such continuities of use, language, pathway, skill
as could be sustained. Nourish the dew, mitigate the intrusion.
And when all was gone, as it would be, he could keep
at least some tracery, some crystalline seed,
some impression or whorled print of what it had been
as nucleus or hint or inspiration
for another corner of some other world,
mental or physical or in-between.
Nothing could be kept, of course: it was all evanescent
as the apricot-lace buttress of bunched and dissolving cloud
spilling now behind oakwood and white-rendered
barn above the red roadsign on the steep corner
where the fence was. None of it was either
physical or mental, it was all both and beyond both
but it was good and it was loved and there was something
founded within its lineaments that made clear
how in its slow, elusive being or non-being
it returned the love and was also a kind of guardian
to those who noticed. And sometimes it seemed the noticing
was more important than both, and would go on.

Rupert M Loydell

OTHER ROOMS

i.m. Peter Redgrove, 1932-2003

Full moon, high tide,
smell of salt in the air;
oceans can seem kind
but a man got washed away.

Windows emit more light
than pale sun gives out:
this was the house
of the laborator.

He owned
a collection of hills,
the secrets of pools,
rich smells and clay ooze.

What he knew
could only be said
in the language of thunder,
seen in sand and stone.

Departing from us
he left books of wisdom
and magic in the world;
many words of blessing.

The future's full of stories
and other rooms, unexplored.
They are in a different country
where we have no choice but to go.

Absence marks the opening of days,
loss grows fainter as the wind
tears his voice away. It is only
truly dark within the cave of self.

Janis Mackay

MORAR

The very few, here this April noon
Bend to shell gaze
Or sit still to wave wish
Or join in salt air kiss
Art I LOVE YOU in damp gold sand
Then smile easy, caught to be remembered
Years hence, on a backcloth of Skye and Rhum.

Or there's them go sullen, scuffing grit rock
Cast into the creel of loss.
'It is as you come that you find it'
says R.L.S.

so, this beach, this whole wide white crested sea
shell sand wind sky
becomes more of itself
the less, and more, I grow.

For now, this April noon
I am white paper rained on
Then dried in the wind.

PRAYER FOR REMEMBERING THE WILD

Sometimes all I can do
Is hold my face upwards
And imagine wild geese flying into the North.

And sometimes, like last Wednesday
When the bluebells could have been
A love blanket and not a fallen birch between us

I heard them pass
Above my below.

There are times when forgetting unmagics the days,
Times when nothing seems wild anymore
And the songs in me fall dumb.

Then they come and find me
Where the wind is hushed and still
And fly over with their call and wing beat
To follow my drum.

These times, when remembering breaks in
I am back standing in vast fields
Intact.

Kevan Manwaring

LOOKING BACK

I walk towards the light
wanting to turn around.

Wanting the night to fade
with the affirmation of your face.
But I must press ahead
and trust you will make it.
That you will slough your shadow –
the snakes at your heels,
and find your way to the door of day.

I strain to hear your footsteps
but they are deafened by my heart.
Love bound blind,
my eyes need proof, but I cannot look.
To doubt, to grow impatient,
and I shall lose your forever.
I must bide my time

and let your wounds find their own mending,
your true feelings to surface.
Yet how I yearn for
this bitter winter to be our spring.
Ah, how slowly rises my bride.
O, to kiss the darkness,
to banish this uncertain silence…

I walk towards the light,
wanting to turn around.

ON VENTRY SANDS

Heading west until the road runs out.
Travelling to stillness.
On Ventry Sands
defeating the King of the World.

Time retreats in this Tir nan Og –
ancient land of the ever young.
Chasing the sunset
to the end of the Old World,
following the moon till morning.

The ocean's susurration
erodes the road's brittle edges.
Here in Dolphin Bay,
where pubs jostle like men at a bar,
we climb singing mountains of the mirror-brine.
Dancing light and shadow
of wave and cloud
that blow both warm and cold –
reflecting the currents of the heart.

Footpaths spiral, grooves in stone,
ruins of cross and sword.
Flotsam of life,
refugees of the western storm,
sheltering on a narrow strand
in ramshackle truck and caravan.

Lost pilgrims gather,
honour friendships
that have made it this far,
and with gaze blessing farewell,
dream the road back home.

Ruth Marshall

THE COUNTRY OF LOVE

My teacher said I should fall in love
at least three times a day.

Sometimes I forget.
Or, seeing no one for days,
fall in love with velvet
or cheese, swallows, or the colour green …

But now
I do not know what country this is.
A stranger
who may be an old friend
tells me, "This is the Country of Love."

I have three types of money in my pockets
But none of them is of use here.

In the market
I gather green things
amazed at what is on offer –
and all of it is good
and all of it is free!

THREE

Three stones can be a gateway.
Three cloths can be a cave.
Three seconds can be an eternity,
And three words speak all the world's wisdom.
Nothing is wasted.

CELEBRATING BRIGIT

Yesterday the women made crosses,
and bound bundled rushes for Brideógs,
dressing them lovingly in rags
torn from an old white sheet.

Today I wake early,
dreaming of my mother,
the road below silent as Christmas.
Snow has made brides of the hedges,
thrown a mantle over the first tender greens,
rounded the corners of the real world,
making VW Beetles of the cars.

Yesterday the women made magic,
humming like bees making honey
to nourish the soul of the world.
They broke bread together
and stepped through the fire that did not burn.

Today I gather fuel in case this weather holds,
tend my own hearth,
fetch water,
write and pray.

OUT OF THE NIGHT OF STARS

(for Cian)

Out of the night of stars
a cord leads
down

Towards
a shimmering egg

Something takes form
begins

is new here
becomes

Host to a secret
link
in a cosmic chain

Is this an earthly prison?

Or the joyous choice
of an unbound heart?

THE LOW ROAD (INIS MOR)

I walk the broken track
down to the cove where Aine swims each day,
my face hard and dry from island walking,
visitor, that I am.

I see them,
giant slug-like, at the water's edge,
and balanced on their middles,
in an asana.
Balanced between the elements,
creatures of earth and sea.

My clumsy foot breaks the silence.
Dog faces turn
to the sound of stone on stone.

Husky, old sea-dogs bark,
belly crawl their way to the waves
and slip with a dancer's grace
into their element.

Blessed by sun,
Blessed by weather
Blessed by hospitality

Blessed by company
Blessed by bicycle
Blessed by comely saints
Blessed by bloody cranesbill
Blessed by wild strawberries
Blessed by sight of seals,
I walk the low road to Kilronan.

Paul Matthews

THE LIVING ROOM

The picture under which my father died
hangs over my fireplace now.

I always wanted it. This eagle on a pine bough
gazing upwards into the round ripe sun.

Always I assumed it was an evening coming on.
But now as I sit here in my own house

I think by his dying he has stitched a subtlety
between the eagle's eye and this red world that's rising,

and I am back with him two summers,
moving his deathbed into the living room.

That is what he wanted – to see how roses
burn in a window within the last word of a looking.

I was reading the Resurrection to him, when suddenly
he stared wildly into the sunlight, and was gone.

CHRIST AS ALPHABET

Him? That's only God,
stepped down from the stars
to taste our vinegars.

That Fool – he scribbled
the one Word he was
into the wordless dirt.
He forgave his enemies!
Omega-and-Alph,

he hung there all afternoon
forsaken by himself.

He was the Word made flesh.

Five vowels howled
through his open skin.
Three alphabets
were crucified with him.

The letter killeth, he said.

Hebrew, Latin and Greek,
binding in their intricate patterns
matters the stars once spoke.

Forgive me, dear Fool, if
with this pen I grave
you in the ground again.

It's only through such a death
that you can rise in our human breath.

THE GROUND OF ARTEMIS

Last September we went to Ephesus to visit the ruined temple of Artemis. My wife's study of such things had prepared her for it. As for me, I wanted honey on my lips. In this temple dedicated to the Word I would ask a blessing for my work in poetry.

It was a Turkish woman with a wrinkled face who eventually swung the gate open. She tried to sell us a map of the site, but we already had one. My wife walked on ahead into the temple grounds. I lingered with the woman as she held out pretty rings and trinkets, coins, dug up from the strata of her ancient petticoats. I could see my wife beckoning from the ruins, but one of the coins had the bee of Ephesus printed on it. This, surely, was authentic.

I handed the woman a note for I don't know how many thousand Lira, and immediately she bend down and wiped it in the dirt, brushed it across her lips, and at last I was free to enter.

My wife, however, intent on us exploring the Mysteries together, had grown annoyed at my loitering, and by the time I caught up with her she was quite unwilling to speak to me. I showed her the coin, but she tossed her head and left me stupid there in the sunlight.

I liked the bee on that coin. I kept fingering it as I wandered alone among the chunks of marble. I have it in front of me now. I can scrape the oxides off with my thumbnail. This is not counterfeit.

And maybe the spirit of that place did loosen the language in me, because a few days later I wrote:

> Only one column remains
> to your temple, Artemis,
> and how glad I am   to share
> its narrow shade this morning
> with two girls two cows
> and a fig tree as your peahens
> squabble in the sun.

Yes, but it was sweetness I wanted, milk and honey – not that angry buzzing in my ear, not that wrinkled creature diddling me out of banknotes.

Who's to say, though, that to be stung in such a place isn't the more authentic? If I were to go there again I would thank the woman for that exchange of currency. And to my wife I say,

> I am ready to go down now
> not knowing fact from fiction
> into the ground of Artemis.

Anne Brayton Meek

RESONANCE

When a vocal sound
Has a focal point

When the very inner core
Is found

When you explore
And you unpeel more and more

When you deepen and depend
On seeking on and on,

You come upon
Something that does not end –

An inner and outer truth.

The proof is in discovering,
The joy is in uncovering
And revealing pure love.

At our very centre –
When you enter with a clear tone –
Love is your own essential essence,
Your own ever-becoming substance.

The Divine within

Sacred fire

Pitching your vibratory rate higher
Yet contained, sustained.
In true love outpouring,

Restoring all within,
Coming out in adoration:

Such is the singing exploration.

DISCRETION

Discretion,
Who's being?
Is it my breath,
Or the one who breathed me?
To identify;
To be at one.

The quality tells,
It is more than perfume,
It heightens,
It awakens.

The breath also,
Breathes the whole body.
You emanate,
But is it cloudy?

It has to be totally pure,
Incorporating a pure heart.

It is gift,
But the inner emptiness
Must be established,
For the Divine breath
To fathom you,
And instil you with bliss.

The mind must be servant
And not too knowing,
Yet knowing
Who empowers.

It is subtle,
But unmistakable.
The Divine presence
Can and does inhabit
Our very gross bodies.

It infuses the soul,
But if you are clear
It plummets into the physical
And you become radiant.
Nectar for all
Who are able to receive.

Jehanne Mehta

from HEART OF YEW

PROLOGUE

If you are afraid to fall,
everywhere is edge and
crumbling:

the puddle where the rubble of
the old road rises;

this spring about to uncoil,
all at once in ripples,
out of bole and bough;

the speckled depths in the eyes
of friends,
when words threaten to open the
gulfs of the heart.

Nowhere is safe now;
we could tumble through anywhere,
without warning,
slipping into adjacent landscapes
we have always inhabited,
but with closed eyes,
between breaths.

Everywhere
we are threatened
with awakening.

CUP

Opaque and foam white
This body lies,
At the moment where the tide meets
The land,
Beautiful as alabaster,
Or the sea smooth stones
Of Atlantic inlets,
Sculpted by the green wave
And the moon.

This is not mine,
This vessel, which becomes translucent
As the tide rises,
And dissolves into limpid light
At the sea's edge,
Containing for an oceanic instant
The whole round world –
Before the wave breaks
And drops it once more
Out of boundlessness,
Onto the gull guarded gateway
Of the solid shore.

This is not mine
This quintessence of frozen flow.
It is earth's daughter, it is
The cup I carry and
The cup that carries me,
Lent to my seeking soul
For a span
To catch the sun and tide of
Transmutation,
To bring forth out of iridescence
The son,
In showers of gold-glistening
Transparent
Blood.

WILD MAN

He took the desert by storm
and he peopled it
with the words he forbore to use
he let them slip away from him
so easily
like a woman who is used to giving birth
he let them slip away
till he was empty
as hollow as the tall dark jars
the womenfolk carry
fetching cool water
to fetch the well water home
and he wore the desert outside in
wearing its jaggedness next to his skin
that wild he was

Before Anthony or Paul
he faced them
the siren the wraith the mirage
and they used his own words
to embody themselves
and they came back to taunt and to jeer
they grappled him down
till his breath was a gasp
and they left him for dead on the hot red stones
stretched out wordlessly
under the desert stars
under the great desert moon
but he rose and he took his own death on his back
gently for fear it might tumble or crack
that wild he was

And the desert turned around then
and looked at him
and she opened her secret door
his scant needs were met
abundantly
and the sun made a nest in his heart
and his words were returned to him
so resonant

the wind was amazed and took flight
in his bones they were humming
in his blood they were thrumming
guiding his feet towards home
and he walked till he came to Jordan's shore
round about and hidden was his pathway there
that wild he was

And he said I will baptize you with water
the waters of the womb he said
but One will come after
baptizing with spirit
One will come after
baptizing with spirit
One will come after
baptizing with spirit
my words are vessels
waiting for filling
vessels
but He is the wine

SONNET

You are so far spread greater than you know:
You track the long trod dismal daily grey,
boned, kerbed and neatly boxed in a clay
border, heart blindfold, not even a toe
out of line, thinking unopened, slow
no wild verges; yoked to the straitened day;
But at the sluice, dreams, thronging the raceway,
Heave at the wet boards, lunging for the flow.

An angel pounds at your temples, stirs your gut;
the sheer light, landing, grips you like a crown.
He cannot bear these streams diverted, channels cut,
and you to yourself dim wasteland overgrown.
Will you turn the heavy winches of this gate,
before the terrible roar of your own soul breaks it down?

EMBLEM

Wear your heart like an emblem, like a banner, like a flower,
Bright on a field of argent, bright on a field of gold.
Carry it before you, like a herald, like a herald,
Like a horn that you are winding as the front line comes on.

Wear your heart like a sun, whose face is unhidden,
Whose rays are like hands that bless although they burn,
Like a joy that is open, even when its petals, falling, drifting,
Dye the plains with purple and its robe is torn.

Wear your heart like a coin of bright copper, that will pay
For every passage you may venture to place your foot upon.
Wear it like a vessel, like a cup that you are sharing,
Though not knowing if your journeying will ever reach a home.

And all the while the river turns,
From the centre to the shore and back
And all the while your beating heart
Is the keeper of the keys.

And all the while the river turns
From the centre to the shore and back
And all the while your beating heart
Is the keeper of the keys.

Wear your heart like a beacon that you raise to rouse the sleepers,
The dreamers in their labyrinths of nerve and blood and bone.
Wear it like a song you will never finish singing.
You know all the earth is listening for your heart's song,
You know all the earth is listening for your heart's song.

Gabriel Bradford Millar

FOR AKHMATOVA

Far from the Neva, and the melancholy
of the old things going,
leagues from the grief of the one
who would not emigrate,
whose lids were at half-mast for
the perpetual funeral of romance,
and the fast passing of innocence –

it is different here:
no snow after Easter;
the birds were muffled by the grave at Komarovo.
Here the drama is domestic.
The heroine is celluloid, and has a hero
who does not die for his truth,
or even live by it.
There is no knock in the night.

No, here the soul is purloined away slowly
by superpowers smiling like saviours.
The craven grab at pleasure has replaced
the noble joy of having backbone,
and the lift of freedom.
For a mess of pottage we have done
what Akhmatova would never do –
we have pawned our sacred essence,
we have sold our song.

FOR IRINA RATUSHINSKAYA

Can we speak for each other?
Can we utter the cargo also
of another's heart?

Here where no common cannon
rattles at the gates…..
where the serpent shimmers
through the marsh of wishes –
even so.
I speak for you,
and you may speak for me.

Who doesn't tussle
with an angel hourly?
Who's not an orphan
sick for home?
Now love has work to do.

THE DELICATE VICTORY

In the torrent of dread
a tiny fire flickers.
I will hold it the way
a two-month old foetus
holds its heart
in its armbuds.

This is the delicate victory.
This is worth all the pleasures
piled in the palace,
and all the lands amassed
by the armies.

SONNET TO JOHN WOOD

The service and the priest dissolved the breach,
And he was with us! John was with us in the room,
And we were woven strong on the immortal loom
Into one fabric, and we each

Knew then that we are held by One,
And death has only a little local gain.

But O! the harp song summoned up the pain
Of seeing one we love set like the sun.

Sorrow saps our pleasure in the rose,
It poisons enterprise and taints the air,
And even friends are far too debonair.

Yet through great grief our holy rescue flows,
And through surrender, though they may not mend,
Our hearts become cathedrals in the end.

Fiona Owen

BECAUSE THE POET

for John Powell Ward

Because of your faith
in language and what
can come through
these marks we make
on white what can shine
enough to stir our matter

because of your faith
in the act of coming here
that saves us from mute non-
being if words can help because
hold this poem up
to the light and

because all this can it can
like a butterfly
flap its wings
and a crack can open
and truth (that word)
can run like some honey-
stuff because

coming here
feels real and something
that we may say yes to
against all that is no
against all that is a raging no
that is a mouth
devouring

and I am small
against it all

but at least
because of
and faithful to
I come here
like you

A MUSING

for Jay Ramsay

The poet meets her muse on the path you know
the one it runs a slender line through bramble
and all kinds of overgrowth dense and wild.
The muse is a kind of child or fizzing stuff of star
a cartwheeling thing *it's about the earth singing
and the clay's testimonies and what mystery brings
out of itself and takes again.* Then with a final *ping*
she's gone like a sprite people once might have believed in.

DOOR

for Mandy

*You will not find the boundaries of psyche
by travelling in any direction, so deep
is the measure of it* – Heraclitus

I tell you about the door I found
in my *self* – creaked it open thinking blood bowels
the usual pulsing matter
stepped onto the sill it was a *precipice*
space yawning around me no edges
my head reeled a moment of vertigo
but then I let go free fall to nowhere
nothing to hurt no landing to make
stars could tumble in worlds
so much inside this one small woman's body

BUDDHA-DOG

your
Buddha-nature shows
through your flow of expression
in daily sleep and wake
ears that listen wholly
to the minute sounds of the everyday
you do not need instruction
in watching breath
to attain focus

eyes whose language
is more eloquent than words
you are awake you are whole
hearted and realised

Buddha-dog I admit
unflinching attachment to you
and recognise the suffering
this brings
                     I do not need
meditation on death, grave yard
reminders of disintegration
                     I am well-rehearsed
in the pain that will come
at your passing
                     I accept this
                     to love you
as I accept all the sufferings
that loving brings

On such a pyre, I will be burnt to ash

I will stand any accusation
of *sentimentality*

bow-wowing low to my dog
in his lovely incarnation

THE SUPPER PARTY

Across the table, the eye-lights dip and flicker.
They are where the meaning is, they are
beams of bright quicker than words,
that weave a web of never-to-be heards so intricate
that the moths are saved their candle fate
by tangle in the thicket.

                 Metal on stone,
                 knife on bone.

The cockerel crows while the crow-types caw,
the pretty tits chirp while the kite-types soar.
Carrion is pecked at, as tidily as can,
but it's the beady eyes that blink out the raw truth,
no matter what the beaks' banter is.

                 Then
                 there comes a silence
which even the shadows shift forward to hear.
                 It is alive with the Unsaid.
                 Eyes in heads
swing left to right, flash dark or light.
                 A cough,
                 a thumb nail chewed,
                 a bite of apple,
there is always the safe focus of food, the fascination
of salt, the simple act of crumbling bread. Claret is sipped
                 too loud, too red.
The Unsaid
     grows bolder as each minute glows to its full height, flares,
then fades to night. It has choked each throat, sealed lips tight
in the very act of clamouring for out.

The head-of-the-table Host scrapes his chair on the flag-stone floor
and stands, his hands turned to above. Like sensing the will of weird,
he waits, perked, for the Word to curl its shape upon his tongue.
                 What can be heard?

The corners of the room; the run of candle wax; the ripening of brie
on the cheese-board.
Then a whisper rustles like the feathers of a bird: "I have been absurd
since twenty two."

(The silence stirs.)

"I have mis-told words for two-thirds of my life. Tonight, I shall be true."

And the Host

raises his glass to the silent supper guests: "For what's to come,
and what's to do."

Rosemary Palmeira

WORLD'S END

There are maps of that old country
creased and stained, prized by a few
there are tokens, markings, clues
however, the dimension is other
the manner of entrance is secret
not lost, hidden nor unknowable.

Even though imagination was paling
the hope of that country persevered
for those who lived underground
there were inklings, reverberations
travellers came with stirring tales
heralds, sirens or holy fools.

*As though from a long way away
as in a dream, as one blind
in the whiteness of snow
I came slowly, believing, unbelieving
I was drawn as though by the summoning
of great bronze bells beneath the sea.*

*All of a sudden it was there – the door
that opens onto the edge of the world
I went through that opening of brightness
as though through a gap in the clouds.*

*And it was all so easy
to be on the other side
it was not possible that there could be
any other place to be.*

*From outside,
all strains towards that dim doorway
all is staked on that one way out;
once there*

you can no longer see how you entered
and it is hard to imagine why
you were not always there nor
how you should ever return whence you came.

So I came into this land of fulness
where laughter is spreading in endless rings
where the Beloved is and the heart's desire
and none of anything else matters at all
for each one is finding his own story
each becoming what he was meant to be.

There strength seized hold of me
and the forgotten skill of sweetness
my wounds became my healing
I came to inhabit my own space
the distances of understanding grew, as
the land pushed out its boundaries in me.

I knew I could stay there for ever
that there was much more, so much!
But soon my body was falling back
unable to hold the vision for long
the grassy land faded away to earth
and the doorway disappeared to the eye.

Yet the taste of that country always remained
and I knew I could somehow return
as effortlessly as the child who dreams
closing his eyes into sleep
and as remote as the breaking of dawn
to the ones who live in night.

Will Parfitt

AND THEY CALL IT HELL

Where he lives is a paradise of abundance.
All the walls are covered multicoloured,
Beautiful patterns, symbols, mandala, Egyptian,
Indian, western cloth, beautiful rich velvet carpets,
All in shades of deep flame which please the eye.
And they call it hell.

The devil laughed until he fell backwards,
Clutching his sides.
Rolled luxuriantly on one of his rich carpets,
His laughter becoming thunder in the heavens.

Clambering over to another hole in the floor, he looked through.
He bellowed. His spit became a torrent of rain below.

He can see a very beautiful woman,
Auburn hair cascading over her shoulders,
Soft but piercing eyes,
Lips made red with swathes of lipstick.
A slight edge of wateriness in her eyes.
She seems to draw him into her dream.

Yes, the devil is dreaming of the pregnant Mary.

THE PRINCESS OF FEAR

I started this day as a small feather.
One side a feathery grey-brown colour,
The other, bands of grey, white, black and blue.
Beneath the black an intense blue slowly faded to white.
I was a very beautiful feather.

Now I am the priestess of fear,
My fresh blood running through arteries,
Grey and white and black and blue.
Blue like the night sky, a royal blue blood.
The black that of a living heart,
The grey, white my own body, the moon.

Under the trees into the holy grove,
My body a quiver of upright hair,
I won't be leaving here till the holes of decay are wide.
I am riddled with worms and moss has eaten my right eye,
When I am no more I will also be myself again.

The heavens, the stars are little, deep purple pink flowers
In a meadow of many rich green grasses.
My legs shake excited as they part,
As they part for my lover, my dark sister, the night.

YESTERDAY I PLANTED AN AUBERGINE

Yesterday I planted an aubergine, today the winter melon,
But she spreads, and demands more room alive than dead.
And now the summoned fishers moist
And all beasts that move on the earth do dwell:
You should eat figs, tasting the juice of your angel.

With the goddess absent, dead leaves are piling, all is deserted,
Yet this receiving is a not receiving, for thou art my lover.
I see you as a nymph with her white limbs stretched by the spring.
Oak of god in thy branches is the lightning nested.
Above you hangs the eyeless hawk:
The full moon, only lovely, flawlessly clear.

For the pine tree, see how green it is. I am here.
My hermitage is thatched with morning glory.
In the midst of all this, a great and high altar forms
With angels beyond count, thousands, thousands,
Ten thousand times ten thousand angels.

THE GRIMOIRE OF TRUTH

I was entering an ancient forbidding town, falling down.
It was beautiful, overgrown, with big stones, like a dream,
The upper stories of all the buildings crumbling.

We go into the place where the place of the earth is woman.
She is a tower of ivory, an enclosed and walled garden,
the magic woman.
Fertile earth mysteriously creating truths.
My grimoire of liberal truth is a tower of sexual strength,
Female and male equal.

I felt strangely empowered by the voice of the ancient being.
Looking deep into the being's large eyes,
I saw the murkiness fade to reveal clear pools of pink light.
Open the gate and let me into the tower
Most people never enter.

Security is a fisheye lens in the door.
A red cross painted against the angel of the lord.
The tower offers security, its castle like shape warming a heart of stone.
For a tower is a song in the heart that is closed to the ears of youth.

I fell to my knees and prayed,
Then walked on silently, magically into awakening.

Mario Petrucci

UNTITLED

With morning those

differentials start
calling again through
static window whose wood-

glass strictures give pause to im
-permanence the same way
speed alters but is not

acceleration or
curvedness can itself
squirm to screw corks of other

dimensions since change is
more than alteration but
flux wallowing in

deeper flux &
i am held here by
such realisation as glass

pressed this moment between
transparency & flow to
frame a kind of

stillness
whose absences me-
rely surface something more

real

UNTITLED

everyone begins as fish &

ends so spiralling after
egg (that other half of our
chains) & setting gills

in gristled knot that buds
legs as tadpoles do & blow-
hole ears halfway down

the back & low-set eye
alien as featherless chick
ah we have peered into

that shared ovum whose
blasto-flesh runs its gauntlet
of fowl & fish so fused at

the tail nothing can be told
apart is this why when i am
late i find in upstairs dark

you on placenta duvet &
hunched round self as wom-
bed ones are? as though i

had just returned from all
eternity in search of other-
self only to catch you

naked & adrift out sleep-
walking space without even
purple navel-twist of rope

to hold you

PRAYER

See the cream of yellow light
rising silent almost as we
watch from dark liquid land

Remember the pucker of first lips
bunching electric roots down
every nervous channel

A mother's untutored head
nodding its degrees
of love

I want to take them
all to the earth

I need to earth them
each in marrow

As I narrow in years
the broadening of longing

How long before
they can no longer fit me

in a box? Let it be
this morning. See me rise
almost

silent in yellow light. Let
land to its yellow roots
part with light

and open to me

Louise Amelia Phelps

THE ONES WHO WEAVED THE WORLDS TOGETHER

There were people who sat in dreaming. At certain times they sat in stillness and fell into silence while they travelled. Casting their dream net to the beyond, they let it fall in points and lines making shapes in the sky. Inside they were timeless, neither within or without themselves but dissolved in the dance.

They cast their net to heal, to make the way safe and soften the passage of difficult things. They dreamed alone and together at special times they only knew – the trees whispered when and the flowers sung the time. Then they would gather in a circle or sometimes they would face the north to catch the rising of a special star.

They dreamed for themselves, for each other, and their people. They kept the worlds close for it was believed that if this was not done, if the people did not dance in dream, the worlds would fly apart, one to the north and one to the south. The worlds would painfully divide and all would be scattered to the dark. They were known as weavers for they wove the invisible threads that kept the worlds together.

In their dreaming they understood much and were met by Shining Ones who helped them on their way, tall and bright they were. They met in the worlds between thought and dream on the other side of a river that could not be crossed . From its silver banks they gave their guidance and their council so the weaving ones could teach. And to the land on their return they sung the songs of what they found, through these songs the Earth found rest, She could dream again.

ETERNITY AND THE STAR QUEENS

The Star Queens said, " Now we ask ourselves of eternity, what is eternity? For moments swim into each other here and a day is but a dream. Is eternity a river that hasn't found it's source? Or is it one that does not remember the rain from which it came, or the earthen door that sung its first liquid breath upon the air?

Or maybe it is the motion inbetween, when memories are lost and thoughts of tomorrow are built on the dreams of today. Perhaps it is the ocean that knows and with endless patience turns the salt urns."

One Queen replied " But I think eternity is found inside a clam shell, that's the place where we can know it. For eternity is the tune that sings a pearl into being, that gathers the grains and spins them golden white. The constant song that sings change into change. But through the flow of the music we are quietened inside, and forget the song for the movement and colours before our eyes."

Jennie Powell

CAVE

No distance from the road the cavemouth sags
Sordid and disappointing –
Not worth the entrance fee. We queue and shuffle:
Handrails and tethered cables, scraps of litter,
Lights and wall-mounted information –
Everything is visible and is visibly nothing.
Bare dirty rock, the developer's chisel
Removing even the prehistory.
But there at the back, beyond the barrier
That bounds the area open to the public,
A narrow cleft half-opens into darkness,
Beckoning how deep? How far?

*   *   *

The drums begin. We blindfold our eyes,
Lie on the floor, together and alone,
And let the drumming take us, throbbing beat,
Sometimes reassuringly familiar,
Sometimes edgy and oppressive. Either way
The sound recedes as we set out to journey…

… I arrive in early darkness. The place is marshy and there's a mist rising like smoke all around – rising from dark water. I find a canoe, kneel in it and paddle. Presently I come to an island in the lake where I land, thankfully on firm ground, and head for the interior, willing to meet a teacher. Plunging through the undergrowth in search of a path I come on a little low hut with a door standing open and a fire in the firepit. There's a very ancient, wizened woman by the fire. I ask her: Are you my teacher for the work with death? What is important for me to remember when doing this work?

She says nothing, turns away and throws sticks into the fire, one small stick after another. Is she saying I'm just a stick? I sense that she doesn't like my word 'important'. In this hovel it sounds pretentious. So I ask: What would I be well advised to remember? – you will advise me well. She says: You don't know who you are, until you've been through the fire.

"What must I remember? I'm so afraid of death, I think I won't remember
anything for fear."
"But you're here."
"Yes, I chose to come and do this."
"That's what's important to remember."

*   *   *

Is the rock singing, or is it the blood
Thrilling our eardrums in the vaulted dark?
We track each other's steps among the bear-scrapes,
The charcoal-heaps, the calcified stream-beds
Studded with inch-high stalagmites. The beams
From our helmet-lamps probe the space ahead.

Bobbing and swaying in their mobile light
The natural sculptures of this temple hover:
Stone waterfalls flowing motionless for millennia,
Frilled draperies of rock, fluted and twisted columns,
Here dyed with warm earth-tones, there glistening
In absolute white purity of a bud just opened.
We tiptoe past with infinite respect
Into still deeper space.
                    Suddenly, jolting,
A human hand-print glows in ochre, then another.
Not-alone made visible shocks our hearts.
Before we can recover, we find more –
A high-domed mammoth looms in southern France.
Here is a bear, there a wild charge of horses,
A pacing stag, a hackle-raised hyena,
Intense aliveness in the pure outlines
So attentively, so worshipfully traced
Among the prompting hollows and projections
Of surfaces three hundred steps from daylight.

Almost afraid our breath, our body-heat
Might harm these works kept safely undiscovered
For thirty thousand years, we leave the cave,
Blocking the entrance, and carry home
A weight of thankfulness and reverence
As massive as the cliffs of the Ardeche.

*   *   *

I went back to the old woman with another question about death. She was standing in sunlight by the door of her hut, slitting a small animal open lengthwise with a sharp knife and gutting it. (It looked like a lizard.) Then I thought she was gutting another animal, maybe a rabbit, more regarded as edible. Next she was cutting up apples and throwing away the core, and my attention was caught by the word core. I was being shown: The bit that you think matters, try to get to, the guts of the thing, the core – she's throwing away. That's not what nourishes you. You've got it backwards, paying attention to and valuing the wrong thing.

I was struggling to understand, and the journey was saying: Don't try to understand this, just be here.

Now I'm standing on the edge of the firepit looking up through the smokehole, seeing the smoke stream upward and escape. And I'm being told: Pay attention to the smoke, the upward movement, the freeing. And I'm thinking I'm not supposed to escape, to get away from the earth. I'm supposed to get more into the body, not out of it. The journey says: Don't try to understand. The old woman says: You've been in the fire all your life. You think there's a hideous ordeal waiting for you at the end, but it isn't so. Life at the end is not any different from how life always is. Don't pay attention to the embers – pay attention to the smoke.

*   *   *

See them – see in near-total darkness
Our forefathers making pictures in the cave.
What drives them to it? Come and look –
See with their eyes.

Squat here among the bones and soft brown dust,
All that remains of many generations
Of bears who used this place to hibernate.
Men use it now. Darkness so thick you almost breathe it,
Relays of torches constantly renewed.
Their light makes homely a ten-foot circle.
Beyond, the vastness weighs exhaustingly
As though the roof needs holding up by willpower.

This place is safe and dangerous at once,
Threatening to crush our spirit, to put out
The light that is our work. Deep in the earth
We long heartwrenched for sun, breeze, flowing water –
For the freedom season when the warmth returns,
When we might even sleep under the stars.

Unable to endure this place without them
We labour to include the animals –
The sunlit ones we vividly remember,
The fast, the strong, the fierce and the prolific,
Making a likeness they can recognise
To fascinate and capture all their spirits
And keep them safe with us. Winter is terrible.

We have the skill to save the animals
If we can draw them breathingly enough
To give them power to stay alive till spring.
We work as hard as this, never to find,
When the time comes again to leave the cave,
A dreadful stillness in the greening wood.

*   *   *

Whatever you paint in life
Whatever you choose
Paint it with care and love,
Wildness and joy.
Paint with all your heart
The definitive self-portrait
Of your humanity.

In the hidden worlds we journey to
We find all worlds are one.
We bring back wisdom and vitality
For living in one world.

Spirit of the drum
Lead us into darkness
Compel us to make light

Jay Ramsay

A SUICIDE BOMBER REACHES THE LIGHT

So where are the beautiful women ?
I have been in hell, where my heart could not breathe
flame racing down the length of the chassis on impact –
the last thing I saw as I buckled to my knees
the slit throat of the stewardess (the one I denied)
and even then, I knew... and then
the most unbelievable blackness
darker than I could have ever imagined
and soft as velvet, falling as I flew

Then the light like a sun came
from as far away as a single star...
and there are many of us, all moving together
and the light became white-robed figures
waiting as if at an Arrivals
and there was one for me, and I cannot tell you
but her face was pure love
and my heart seized –

I died again there in her eyes.
My mind flooded with that sunlight
then I woke. And all around me, the others who had come
being tended to, as I watch them
(one still holding his mobile phone)
in their soul bodies and their grieving
made of the same substance – and then I knew
where it all went wrong, and how
my future now lies with each one of them.

They do not speak Arabic here
they don't need any earthly language
these beings speak with their eyes, mind to mind,
and most of all, straight into the heart –
and this appears to be some kind of hospital

but outside, as in a field of white
and there is a path between two hills
where some are already walking.

I cannot recognize anyone, but everyone I see
is already familiar to me
you will probably not understand this...

As for you, Mulla Omar, you didn't understand anything
and the text you gave us is a lie:
there is no Prophet here, sitting in judgement
all there is is Love, and naked souls
waking out of their shock and pain
and loving souls who sit with them, and guide them:

All there is is Love – and what she says is
it can be mine again if I choose it.

from ANAMNESIS – the remembering of soul, 3

written as poet in residence at St. James' Church, Piccadilly

What is the gift of your life ?

Beyond naming, an utterance
in your throat's depth, your soul's
intention to live –

Can you recall it ?
You sit in meditation, surrounded by stars.

What are you living for ?
There is an answer so personal
so passionate, beyond all conceiving
in your innermost coding –
that your secret may die with you,
but not before you've had the chance
to witness its luminous traces.

And she, he is your answer
that other one nearest of all within
who shines in you like an icon, a sun.

What else is there ? The spiral climb
hearing your name called through the mist,
ever-stretched towards your blue potential
true self's surrender, that is the only way home.

from ANOTHER COUNTRY

for Lara away in California

6.
The warmest flame.
Love circulating to love
becoming more love,
waking as you sleep
sleeping as you wake.

Welcome to our 24 hour day
this must be God's country
circling its ever-broadening perimeter.
Finally in the centre, the earth is turning
as we are supposed to see it –

And between two points on the map
among a myriad of lines veined dense as flesh
but electric, we travel, we connect in seconds,
we sip each other's nectar like hummingbirds

where they fly free, in your country.

7.
You can say what you like
you can try to fit in
but all that really matters
is that you play the music you love.

Dawn to our waking.
Every bird singing as it does...
I want to open the window so you can hear them.
All that matters is you play
the music you love.

And when you do, amazing things happen.
Tears, relief, deep imagination
within your expression of love.

When you play the music you love
what happens is the work of love
the whole air become intelligent love.

THE FURTHER REACHES

1.
in every small London town

What is it like disappearing?
How is it accomplished? In the silence
we can only imagine, and fail imagining –
70,000 of us this year, it says.
The lift glides down.

You wonder if we don't just dematerialize
at a certain frequency, bent on disappearance
or is that a body they've found in the canal?

And still its inhabitant has vanished.

Darkness. The further reaches.
Voices in hell singing in the park.
If they weren't so dark, it would be music.
On the edge of the wind, it almost is music.

Then the rain turns them to silence
with its simple switch of water. Depart!

2.
on the Seventh Day

The emptiness inside everything.
The hollowness. Did you know it was there?
The sheer spaciousness—how can you explain?

Nothing is close-up anymore.
Everyone is preoccupied. But nothing is filled.
Everywhere you look. The motions. The attitudes.
Predictable enough. But even the closest to you
are feeling it. Not saying it. Quite.
But wondering *actually, what is there to do?*

Tomorrow's newspapers already waiting
full of yet more noise and vacancy
spread to pass an empty day

3.
a new country

It's when a man gets up
and disappears, walking out of his life
as if up the length of a hidden country lane
years before when he first thought of it
walking away he doesn't know where
but forward, and further
leaving it all behind
feeling his shoulders free and weightless

becoming light, and silent (above all)
the peopled world turning into space
a white land that should be green and wild
(and maybe also is) but is white
as the hollowness inside everything becomes it

and it's here I can forget what I've been told
who I'm supposed to be, and what I think
and the words I seem to have to use
all of it can fall away, and all there is to do
is to Be and Listen (oh yes) to something quite new.

Angie Rawlinson

DASH THE SKY

You
are as far away
from where
i am
as i am
far away from the star
i just saw

fling its sparkled light across the dark night sky

A rocket?
a shooting spray?
someone on their way
to heaven?

or
my wish
my inspiration
travelling as lonely as

i am here
wondering
where on earth
are You?

DOVES 111

I will live alone somewhere – maybe out at sea
far away from smog and whirring sounds
tarmac and stiletto heels

I will have a garden filled with cockleshells
and hanging from the branches of the sycamore tree
bells will chime as the breezes breezed
until a wind blew a storm over head

I will shelter inside the wooden hut
held together with bamboo
and mats of flaxen hair
spun from the strands
that malt
within sleep

And you may visit three
four
times a year
and we will lie under
the huge star ridden sky
and tell each other stories
to amaze and thrill our souls

And we may dance through our darkness
allow feelings
to rise
and fall
as the waves do
along the shoreline

Ben Rayner

SO MUCH

So much life and love
for one mere mortal being –
to hold the sweetness of the earth
in the palm of your hand,
to fling your arms wide open
and embrace
the vastness of the sky,
to caress the sea
with silken fingers,
slip down
into soft blue depths,
to be washed by the sun
and kissed by rain.

To let the storm howl
through the cracks in your soul
and fling itself
with fierce abandon
into the corners where you hide
and prise the tendrils of your fingers
from the safety
that you think you hold
rip you free
and send you
flying.

To listen to the drops of water
trickle down
through moss and ferns,
quiet reflections
of light and cloud,
become a part of all things wild.

Sit upon a mountaintop
so far from the place that I was born,
yet so much more a place that's home
than any other place
or time
I've known.

VANISHING POINT

As early morning mist
that melts into the trees,
as shards of golden light
dancing on the sea,
as warm and steamy breath
vanishes into air,
as rising smoke that twists and turns
and finally disappears.

The point from which the snowflakes fall
when gazing to the sky,
the place to which the sound returns
after the gong is struck.

The little voice that whispers,
the fire joining black,
the point at which horizons meet
when no limit has been set.
The playful way the laughing wind
turns and lifts the dying leaf,
the point from which all teardrops fall
that southward flying geese
echo with their call.

The ever widening circle
on the surface of the pond,
the place to which we'll all return,
when we can call it home.

Peter Redgrove

NIDOR OF NINE JUICES

The blended smell after sex,
       the usufruct in the skin,
            the orchard
In the skin, or as the rose melts
       its odour with the violet,
            climbs out of our skin –
It is our invisible child
       who looks out through
            nine windows times two,
The perfume-casements of our solo chest,
       the access buttons that shine
            like stars in the hug
Of our shirt enclosing us; the hand
       seen plainly laid across the back;
            this very marine sex
Is best wallowed in;
       meditating in the yoni of the Goddess,
            the glisten
Seeps slowly like a blessing
       bestowed from above
            and covers you with that
Flexible garment of juice,
       sitting on a ripple that is inward,
            you are then
Gorgeously robed in excitement,
       a slow electrical waterfall;
            the pulses shining,
Or japa of elixir,
       the tap-tap on the head
            of clitoral distillates
Of the universe, the white source
       just over the head, the robes
            soaked in moon-juices.
One lives

in the whole dome of her then,
                              there are
The movements that tenderly
            apply themselves everywhere;
                              strange countryside,
The lawsuits and penalties swiftly cancelled
            like a grassfire on a mountain
                              and the charred places healing
as though nourished
            by the nine fluids
                              in the rain.

AFFAIR

The ritual of turning into a wet girl,
            in wet clothes I am a woman,
                              multi-orgasmic
With a big yoni-shirt,
            a big bright Vee hanging
                              between my bosoms
Because she encloses
            a portion of the universal space
                              which is wet like a pot
Or the meditation hall inside a lily;
            rain creating meditation clothes
                              all over the body;
She transfers zest to all my organs,
            I laugh with the fragment of Zeus
                              lodged in my head,
There is gold ruched under her armpits,
            my cry is berserker, creating
                              a large movement
Of swamps and woods
            where the veil is thin for both of us;
                              on the glass mountain of sweat
We come together
            like two cats
                              lapping at the same milk –
Sleep: entering the mountain.

GHOSTLY TOWN

Among the evening
       smells of Falmouth,
              the metals wafting
Off the river-mud
      like invisible foil unpeeling,
             shaking in silent thunder,
A time which snaps
      the briar-bush of clock-hands
             while the Cornish stars
Take up their positions
        slowly rising
            in the night-time skin
Of every visitor
      in her newfound bedroom.
            What town is this
With frozen seconds?
      The lovers achieve it,
            their actions stop the clock,
A big shining
      glides across the water,
           slides into the dock.

AWAKENING TO THE LIGHT

(for Su Bainbridge)

You are, you generate and you radiate out a light so bright I cannot look. It effervesces in your eyes and sparkles in your hair. It is the joy that spills from your mouth: it is so huge, you cannot name it or contain it.

Your heart commands the arts and alchemy of transubstantiation: you clap your hands and that which was dull, muted and monochrome bursts into shimmering, vibrant colour. Pigeons fly swooping from their pigeonholes. Chess-pieces paint out their squares and put on their party clothes.

Even grumpy kings and stand-offish queens are charmed by your joy. You make every round peg feel itself safe and snug in a round hole.

Your light flows as a sea to every river, to every tributary; and reaches even me.

Beside you grey shadows retreat to the grey cupboard where they belong.

Your light infects me. I absorb it in osmosis: shed rotten layers and cast off ancient impositions.

You are light; and your light is simple and bright. It's clarity, concise: transcending the muddy convolutions of intellect. Your wisdom is being, simply being.

There are degrees of light and degrees of shadow; and each is a truth, irrefutable, unto itself. The truth you have chosen, the truth that chose you, the truth I now drink is clear, sharp and painfully beautiful.

From this vantage point, I see what you see: I see beyond the cities, beyond the clouds, beyond the sky; and below me a zen landscape of mountains and sea, a calligrapher's tree burning bright with vertigo.

I am dizzy with the knowledge that there can be no more fear of falling.

You are light. You are love. You are everything that is easily mocked. The vocabulary of your goodness is without sophistry. There is no ironic post-modernist, no educated fool, no surgeon of cool who can cauterise or analyse what simply is.

They may have an army of lexicographers and have built a causeway of shifting shadow

– they may have constructed, in the moon's thin glare, a mythology of undeniable intricacy – they may dazzle with their erudition, but you know and I know and they know, they are without conviction.

Their darkness, their ennui, their desolation is as familiar to me as you are strange and new.

I want to be possessed by you.

I want to ride over this fear of descent into platitude, of speaking my light in idiot Christian tongues.

I ask myself can I let go and just be?

I know the blood-red hard wood: it has the familiarity of skin; it is as known to me as these veins, this flesh, this brittle pale bone.

I have torn myself with chainsaws, chisels gouges, rasps. I have smoothed my mouth with fine grade sandpaper and cast a perfect web of poetry and deceit.

I apprenticed myself and am now master, but I ask, can I let go of such conceits?

It has been a long mountain track, littered with numerous ragged, unrealised abortions: each with the attendant pain of childbirth. I have the scars, look! But, now, here, I can turn out carvings of perplexing, savage complexity; smooth to the touch; slick as machined metal; hard, erotic, beautiful – beautiful in the limitless darkness.

I am frightened by this dexterity: my unthinking dedication to the glorification of shadows and skin.

You are light; and in your light, my shadows are but dismal, futile mutterings. The light in me has woken from a yawning, protracted sleep; and I am shocked upon waking, to find my temples – for all the years and careful craft – standing stark, glittering and glorious, in a war-zone of craters and ash.

You are light. Your truth has overwhelmed me. The darkness no longer hypnotises, for all its contrivance and trickery. Its mystery, its fine-fingered ornamentation, has dissipated into the commonplace and ordinary. It may master the thesaurus, but it no longer masters me.

You, my love: I enter into your light, in humility. I have no maps, few words and just the basic tools of a small child. Speechless and blundering, with my sophistry in ashes, I anticipate a happiness that surpasses understanding.

Alan Rycroft

OCEAN

Ocean, you are so much
Like life and death,
Image of the void's fullness,
Origins   before the first explosive
Pinpoint of fermenting flame
Before the stars and stillness of the suns
Whirlwind and the wheels of form
Perturbed the pure pristine of the unborn
Potencies of presence that
Gave birth to us   some slimy molecular spawn
Out of the murky deep
Suddenly emergent from a womb of
Sand, to slither and slide in rock pools
And the drained mud of the land.

And now in our evolved
Barbarian sophistication   how we flock to you
When the sun walks lucent
On bright waters
To renew our primal wedding bonds in wonder
And festival the memory
Of vows first taken
When the word was young
And almost meant what it said;
When men took oaths upon the heart
There were no holy books
But only what was written in the forests and the skies
Where pledges rang in wonder
And prayers prayed themselves
And echoed wayside shrine to shrine
With the songs that sung
Of dreamtime and the years.

And in a mood to come again
Into the outer precincts of the mystery

With contemplative heart
We bow down to blue infinities
Go yonder to the borderless land
We come from
To the arms of a limitless love,
Baptise our children
With no name
Go naked in the fiery font
Of a summer's day
When every man is Adam
Before the Fall
Paddling in presence;
Our worn and wearied feet
Tired of the trudging, these heavy heartlands
All our long and labour days,
To slake our land-lubbered bodies' thirst
To be fish again.

That memory is a holiness
And communion
Though we moderns don't see it that way,
Our very education is a stripping away
Of earth and sea of their gods.
But to be once more in your body
Is to break the bread of being,
And we swim not in salt solutions but
In the arms of a majestic and
Mercurial mother
Whose embrace is a kiss
Of purging peace – the gentle scintillation
Of the sheer rejuvenation –
Or – we are in a sudden
Taken without warning,
Our flesh fish food and broken
Where there never was anyone
All gone with the god's first word and
His last into the emptiness
Of the fathomless deep.

2.
And we honour this:
First kinship with the sea
The sheen on our burnished bodies

Is the grace of the unknown Michelangelo
Who pummels and shapes
This rough clay DNA
So tangible to touch and tang of taste
And sight; erodes our granite heart
As we glide and glee
Upon the waves and are free
To be, to dip and dive and sport,
Even bring all manner of
Small ingenious instruments
And gear for going deep
Into the deep, and ships
Of all manner of shapes
And methodologies of motion,
Spawn of our hard-wired brain
To spice the play.

Though this Machiavellian module of
Strive to survive whatever,
Where every soul must grapple
With every other
In the blood-red arena
Of ever more total colonization of the
Mother, cannot really conquer you –
Though it damn well tries,
Flies the skull and cross bones
This mind marauding, with mechanical claws
Upon your surfaces,
Raids the hold of the void vast deep
To make a booty of your bounty.
But like space you shall outbe
All beings   you are the god-zone
Property of no-one.

We are water of your water
Solid seeming as we are
Fluid animations drawn by an
Invisible light   we do not know
Or see; echoes, resonant shadows
Of the musical mystery.
Yet some reality more real
Enacts itself in us, in the ceaseless weave and
Interweave and meshing of the waves,

Everyone a note never to be repeated
Of the ocean's ceaseless symphony.

Though we are but mirages
In the desert of time
We bear a code too subtle
And fantastical to completely crack –
There's meditation and the maddening
Perplexity, the reason and absurdity…
Your salt within the rivers
Of our blood
Preserved us through the patterning
That stirred and ladled cell-song
From the cauldron of the ages
Midwifed the mad and mutant mind
That real that we do not know
Reaches – and its flowering is us –
To waken as itself
From slumber in the nightmare dream
Of history, and gather
From the contest and collisioning of waves,
The play of ceaseless crest and trough
That dissipates in spray
On the tumultuous shore,
One whole, hale and hallowed
Of the sea.

3.
Some say as we burn
Last of the earth's black blood
Slash and tear her hair
Slice and gouge her flesh
And crush her bones,
The very air we breathe
Shall be our fever
And you shall rise again
From the dying of a world
In the throes of the nightmare
Of its inordinate dream,
That this finite earth
Could ever fill
The insatiable belly of desire,

And like a mother sore abused
By the children she has borne
That came like rough intruders
To their own house,
Her ripe clay gifted moulds
Fashioned for the seeding of their souls;
Some day she may retract the gift
The spendthrift generosities of grace
Once gave, and engulf us.

Yet like the soul
The mind's profound
In the deep you   are   only you
Moveless, immensely, imperturbably,
Forever out of range of the wind
And at the core
Not a ripple of the storm
Of birth and death may penetrate.

You cleanse and absolve us still
Heal us with your minerals,
Yet you receive it all:
The toxic waste of thought
And thoughtless ways,
The casual excrement of poverty
The soulless excess of the rich
And that rapacious paucity of spirit
That is the single root
Of the billion-fold cries of all the earth,
As we drill and trawl
To dearth and death
The playful inexhaustible benison of the sea.

You are primeval power of purity
Symphony of many waters,
Empty of a single sound
Or stealth and shadow of a ship,
Long before the pirates roamed and preyed
And the febrile ephemeral fleet
Of our fragmented mind was lord.
But now we poison you to your bowels
Your dolphins and your whales
We hunt and net and spear,

Our ravening axe within a hair's breadth
Fells the whole tree of creation.

Superefficient hunter
No known predator except his own,
We have forgotten and forsaken
First kinship with the ocean,
Soul surging freedom and
The sea-shantying heart,
Passion always poised upon the surf
And after every momentary sway
And loss of balance, stronger still
To mount, and ride the waves again.

Stood thus between the final deluge and
Inertias of the robot blind
Perpetuation of all we have been
We do not know ourselves,
We grope as in a room without light
Crashing into objects dimly seen,
Tying ourselves up in knots
In wires of our own machine.
Our natural language – prayer
Has become a foreign tongue to those
Struck dumb imploded on the
Unfelt grief of all the earth,
And so must wait upon the miracle,
Turn around, and downside up,
Or go under, and drown,
To be delivered perhaps
By the winds and many waters.
And when the floods recede
We shall come upon a new land.

Karen Eberhardt Shelton

WHOEVER I AM, I AM WITH THEM

You don't know my light
this light from here
its long reach, the myriad confusions
of shingle, high tides and rock bunkers all the way
across the Bristol Channel to the equivocal cliffs of Wales

You don't know what I know, since you are not me,
and why I speak in the way I do
about those chalk faces, that cloud formation
the twigging branch outside my window
flattening in the gushing rain

To birth my poem I walked up these narrow stairs
into a confusion, and there I strive
I offer, make do with old lovelorn timbers, a little whiskey

Grateful birdsongs – another day!
I am not an anarchist.
Do no harm

I am the dusty figments on that painted wing
I and the mushrooms insects wildflowers snails lichens moss
the same chemistry

I am merely the seam
the ragged edge, the lacquer-plated finish, the lymph
slime mud, integrated flora and wings
fluttering around that primal burst of form
I am singing for the salvation
of everything

SMALL PRAISERS OF LIGHT

A lone bird sings in the dark lungs of early morning
as though it loved the world and all the twigs
and leafless trees, sodden grass and mud and frost
and even the coming of yet another grey day.
As though eternal bugs had been promised
or birdseed from the woman in the house.

All they do when the black veil rises
is shout with joy.
As though being alive was electric.
Unrepeatable.
Holy.

Nothing more to do than sing.
The flute of life, the world, the great
underbelly of the humming universe wrapped up
inside a bird

DREAMER'S RAIN

I am gently going under
down into rain
sloping off the roof
in murmured droplets

A paradigm preparing me
to dream
to remember all things
that I know
backward into the lush green
earth and its rounded body
so like a woman
dressed for herself
in lime lace
plump skin calling
to be caressed
for its luxury of clefts
and fern pockets

Rivulets and streams rinsing
this body clean
so its mysteries can be plumbed
by the willing
by the way I feel running
to meet this emerald
that exhales mist
this beauty that loves
the soft drumming
of certain waters

ANIMAL DREAMS

I have a fantasy about lying down
in a field or thicket surrounded
by a herd of deer
and being warmed
by their bodies
and sitting among them reading a book
while they graze without speaking

I dream that I tiptoe
into a bear's den and curl next to his belly,
while his furry arm slides around me
and we hum together in the feral darkness
like contented twins

On the summit of a windy hill
the vastness of forest and river gorge and sky
compose the Bible of Life
as I stand watching at the invisible barrier
with meadow grass and flowers
swallowing my feet

I long to go there not as *other*
but merely myself as *one*
of them

Henry Shukman

LEAVING EL DORADO

I

On the roof of the Hotel las Americas:
first, he's woken by a whine squeezed
from a dog straining to scratch an ear.
Second, a mud of mango skins in the gutter below
raises a cool palm of scent, presses shut his mind's eye.
Third, his shirt beneath his back, a parchment
hot and cold, wet with the ink of travel.
Fourth, a taste of metal in his mouth,
a gum-foil airport tang, the homeward bit.
And fifth, an eye opened on the vultures above,
ash flakes from an old fire moving like flies
under a hotel ceiling, moving, moving.
Lastly, a shroud pulled over the land,
white mist, the winding-sheet of his return.

The trip to Correo Central. Nombre? Pasaporte?
He shoved the scuffed booklet under the bars.
Slickhaired man clicked away. Two minutes
of nameless worry. The boots of men in line
whispering to the marble floor, the ceiling's
murmured answers. Firma, se-ñor – and the letter
was his, gaily fringed, skyblue, light as air.
Dear Johnny, I know this is the worst
time but it would mean so much.
We've all been waiting, of course.
You expect a relief but it's a shock.
Each day so fragile. We're thrilled
about what you're doing. But come home.

His last day. The city waxy-quiet. His farewell
came from the birds, who floated down drawn by his pallor,
cut yearning spirals through the afternoon
until the black wings made the dust jump.

Feet clutched for parapet, wings elbowed
to half mast. Mouths open like dogs after a run.
They eyed him – one eye, bead cut from a rosary –
then, flick, the other eye. Flopped off the parapet.
Waddled close. Sensed his warmth. Waited.
Nuns huddled round a bed, three of the hooded.
And what was his last wish? To rise,
shoo them back to the sky, their seal-bodies
tugged up, sideways, upwards, a city shaking off
its pigeons, then down for a last diurnal beer.

Out through the coralbone polis in a chromespun
bus engined by crackling tomtoms, blare
of trumpets, to a beach's tarry gleam.
The slap and sigh of gelatinous waves
soothed him (grey limp things here too).
Silk-skinned hand to the cooler, the shutter
slid back, sunlight breaking into a thousand grains
in the arsenal. Wet ring stamped by the trophy
of travel on boards roughsmoothed by salt.
Then the levered gasp, the toppled helmet,
the white foam of blossom rising from the stem.
He thought of hay meadows, the August
stubbleland of home. Raised the bottle to them.

The old rose sheathed in the leather Pacific.
He too would fall like the sun, a slow fall,
a ball roped down from the sky, a colossal
thing losing air, shrinking, becoming limp
finally, an empty sack. That was the meaning of return
he would first discover (the other two to follow):
Raleigh's sacks of fool's gold mocked at court,
the fabled crystal city nothing but smoke of a nomad's fire.
The golden things you ferried home became rock,
so much dead weight in the cargo,
once you pulled them into the other daylight.
Perhaps you could foretell it now in the sea's lap.

Then night, the magician's cape flung over the city.
From back alleys, from cheap new avenues,
from tree-upholstered hostels, one-room bars,
rose the tinkle of glass, the flare of brass,
the clink of pieces of eight, of thaler,

dollar, crown and shilling, of hoarded coin
and ingots raw, unhallmarked, sterling
fresh as milk in the frothy pail.
And the windows framed in gold, the doorsteps,
lintels, screens and posts all plated, leafed
and gauzed in gold. And rhomboid gleam of bars
paving the street through which flickered
drinkers' shadows and glitter of dancers' arms
sprayed with the dust of the Gilded One.

Who found it first? Bohlwinkel, Heinemann,
Van Duyper's men come down from Santa Marta?
Juan de Vega, preacher of the farmers
stranded on his Orinoco island
with a thousand men, a thousand dreams
of chicken caldo, foxes and sheep, plucked
down to three by flies, by boas, arrows and heat?
Ortega's troops, steel men on bannered war machines
that sucked hoof holes from crude-oil trails
and devastated the green-sailed canals of ants,
who climbed through playgrounds of bats baffled
into company with thrush-sized butterflies?
At night they raised their trunk of smoke to ward
away the jaguar's cough. Then passed through the clouds
onto the highlands.

                    Parklands of the Lord,
one said. Declared another: La Canela,
Land of Cinnamon, outlying province
of some great kingdom: the Kingdom Guiana
with its stones mortared in gold, its books leaved
with gold and inked with iguana blood,
its golden gutters sparkling in rainstorms,
and shawls of woven gold on beggars' shoulders.
Gold dust would drift from the smoke of its fires.
Soon as they marched they'd see it on the ground.
But all they found, in Bacata, was the lake
Guatavita where once, some said,
a prince with golden skin had swum.

Sir Walter was to find it first, much later,
in his Tower cell at four o'clock
on a January afternoon when it had rained,

when he could hear the slush of gutters dripping,
the slow reviving of bird calls,
the ravens cawing on the lawn below,
and cries of bargemen on the silver Thames
who pulled their boards at Southwark.
Four squares lit up softly, quickly, on the stones
above his desk: four golden rectangles:
he saw it at the end, a wall of gold.
He wore a smile for Beth, his wife,
when she came to kiss his cheek.

His two tall houses were first to float on the stream.
"Blousons today," he told Lieutenant Keymis,
smelling the heat. "By nightfall we'll be gorged
on chocolate!" His first pass on the Orinoco.
He'd caught the Players before he left,
some ignoble yet touching piece.
And in the morning fastened up his crew
by Wapping: then silken down the estuary,
bound for the brassy heart of the world.
That morning entering the forest portal
he felt the shadows trail his unwashed face,
heard unseen fauna rasp and hoot and shriek
and knew at last a back gate had been found.

What did he find? A milkwhite glittering rock,
the oro madre; a mist in the trees –
smoke of some great city's fires? A roar
as of a marketplace, of carts on cobbles,
a thousand vendors – just a falls
plumefalling down a cliff from the clouds.
Then chased down by cascades he glided
back to the lazy barbaric ocean.
Trading beads for golden trinkets, he drifted
back to court, pressed his queen for ships
towards an alliance to make Spain weep.

II

Domingo. Bars chaste, closed like shells,
the town a childlike empty playground
washed of its weekday sin. Then Monday:

the brothels open up their stable doors,
the cavities in fortress walls
fill with the gold of barlights and rum,
and lemon-sellers roam the streets,
and men who wheel the blocks of steaming ice.
Whirring maracuya, melon and pineapple
froth in stainless steel, static cracks
from the ice, cans gleam on counters
where dozy-eyed men in thin shirts,
newspaper on knee, suck on twin straws for lunch,
mesmerized by the motions of the fruit men.

Dawn on Tuesday: the day of travel.
The clouds have lifted in the night.
A hand of shadow blurs the blind.
Outside, below, ribbons lie along the street
tied to the feet of plaza trees.
A dog tugs at something in the gutter
slowly, methodically, eyes lowered from the sun.
Into his bag he packs the spare shirts,
the wool socks, the nights in the sierras,
the daybreaks by saltlakes, the cinnamon coffee
on a cold morning in a smoky hut,
beer shining after a hot river day,
the shrewd geometries of pyramid and plaza.

Now is the time. He thinks of Ricardo,
his new friend and, he still believes, with a shiver,
his lasting friend. Who stammered, "B-b-buenos,"
each morning when he bought his cigarettes and pop,
who with a nod, a smile, invited him to the bullfight
in the makeshift fairground stadium. His face
glistened from too many beers – they sat in Sol –
and from peeling oranges with a penknife for his wife.

Ricardo would understand: a man must go home.
No matter what he has done or left undone,
no matter how little awaits him or how much.
Ricardo would smile, nod, offer him a light.
Fondly they'd drink a beer, clasp hands.
That was the way in the world of leather and wood,
sweat and beer. That was the way a man could be
if he woke each day to one of those dawns:

the hesitant then alarmed rooster call, answered
by an old man's coughing from the church tower.

In this land at dawn you might hear a desert wind blowing,
sounding like summer thunder very far off,
while a blue crocodile of sierra lay somnolent,
secretly vigilant, on the horizon.
You might soon be hot as you walked
under a sky the same blue as the icing
on wedding cakes in panaderias, the blue
of sitting-rooms bluewashed for Christmas.
This was a land in the morning where nothing
spoke to you save those things: the whispered
explanations of the wind, the sun's sermon
the humph, the sigh of hill-dogs settling themselves,
and somewhere sometimes a breaking of water.

Where he was going were other dawns,
of draughty cassock, of voices rising
like tubes of glass in dark places.
He had thought about this, how you could
look at a boulder here and see in it
the same hard crystal of cathedral voices.
What was that thing in both, so hard, so clear?
Why, when you heard it, saw it,
did it make you reach into the day ahead
to take its heart in your hands?
Why did it hush you? And did the birds hear it?
They too tipped up the glass yards of their throats
to drink the arrival of the new day.

Other things to pack: a map, whitened at the creases:
the quilt of his journey coming unstitched.
Biro rings round some names: Chachapoyas,
with its battle-ark grounded on the hill.
Arequipa, the ice volcano Misti
standing guard over nuns walled in white.
Cuzco, Lima, Ayacucho: threaded
on a red wire, the same wire that fed out
from home, now making a loop like a rabbit snare.

A tube of Uvistat 15 – the remembered smell
of Brittany beaches, his mother's hot fingers

spreading the grit and butter down his arm.
The sierra sunlight, a stake that struck and stilled
the quivering unsure thing in one, turned you
into a man with one purpose at a time.
A stiff blue shirt, the kind the Bolivian miners wore,
a coastline of surf stained on the back –
the hotel woman would have scrubbed it out
with a brick of green soap had he stayed another day.
Shirt of his travels, of a man
with cigarettes in breast pocket, who wore boots
and shaved on Sunday mornings. Its cloth
only a little tougher than his skin.

III

Raleigh's son sailed with him second time: lost
to swordsmen on the Caroni; and Keymis:
lost too, to axeblows from a canoe; himself:
mutinied, hauled back in chains, a pipe
of ashes in his mouth, palsy in his bones.
Sonless, queenless, shipless, homeless:
berthed within the Tower, his third trip oared
by quill alone. He steered the treacherous
Oroonoque stream with half-closed eye,
by candlelight, and put his case before
the world: he all but met the Tivitivas,
raven-men whose cities hung in trees,
all but kissed an Ewaipanoma bride,
whose eyes shone between her nipples,
whose mouth chewed corn above her navel.
Even received a golden bead from a Manoan porter.

He knew the geography, the street scene,
drew maps to show us round: the great lake,
Lake Parima, nourisher of the capital,
from whose body the Orinoco flowed.
Temples, palaces, courts of gold, the gilded
avenues - he illumined their walls with his tallow flame.
Colleges, academies, the youth of Albion
side by side with Manoan youth: a westward freight
of Ovid, Virgil, Pindar, maths, an eastward
of gold, coffee, chocolate handed about like loaves.

Grain for gold, gold for Horace, for Homer the brown leaf:
And Virginia ruling Empress of both worlds.
But not yet, not yet: the colours of his maps
ran in London's rain, his logs, his plans all dulled
in Cheapside fog. And himself, stretched
on the block. Neck of the last seeker.

IV

Then rising above the rooftops,
above the upturned washing bowls,
the ghosts of hung laundry, rising
until he sees the tile-mosaic of city roofs,
can see what it all means: a plain of bone,
the city subterranean in grey sleep,
and rising further, in tandem
with the rising sun – red tongue on waves,
bleach water poured into clouds,
peaks tossing gold hair in first light –
he sees this world grow small,
harden into an old fruit.

The homeward bit – he moves his tongue:
leaving this land now, sealing it under the clouds of home.
He follows the gulf-stream trail of jetsam –
weeds, seakale, broken gunwales – across the sea,
a lizardscale river of detritus, oily,
something of old seagull wings disarmed on a beach
and stale cabbage by a kitchen door –
a slow goods train, what floats of the New Indies
to the old country, to the shores of Scilly
where they lift their cargo of nutrients into the rain,
feed displaced peach and raspberry – jewels among leaves
to which a girl in nightie stretches on dewy toes.

A screech and groan of sky: a steel meteor
tearing the clouds above Raleigh's ship.
The riven Atlantic: he looks up from his chains.
Then silent on a curb at Heathrow:
the enclosed land now.
A gust of bus smoke, a frost of breath,
growl of taxi, attack of horn-blast, brick

upon brick above. Families concrete-borne,
behind misted hot windows,
into the gasp of the city.
You feel its sigh on your cheek,
ghost freight of the wind,
coming graceless off grey fields and slates,
off the fallowlands of the soul.

Penelope Shuttle

IN AUTUMN

A sky second to none
knows how to talk in moonlight

The moon, in command of all the ships,
doesn't care

Up there in the dark?
My spirit parcel-post

Clouds fall by the wayside
in an autumn late to begin and slow to end,

the world turning in all its brutal élan

DREAMER'S DREAM

Hidden in the garden grass,
I found a tiny replica of our house

That same night
I met
a rose-red rabbi half as old as time

Child of September,
pupil of rain,

my shoes kept walking downstairs
on their own,
carrying the world out of the world

I learned about China in simple pictures
I used my water-hand to sketch your river,

allowing light
to travel as fast as it liked –

Then came a little marvel summer,
such as I never dreamt

FLOOD

When the Naktong river
floods the town of Pammori

on the waters
comes a box of masks and props,
a playscript

As soon as the townsfolk,
drenched but purposeful,
perform the play,

the waters abate –
But what the play was about
no one remembers –

A pig hunt?
A wedding?
The afterlife?

Pauline Stainer

FLOODING IN THE OLIVE ORCHARD

We hardly noticed it:
water rising in the grass
a silent flooding in sunlight.

Not memory but revision;
time waylaid
by things that never surface

olives throwing back their silver,
bees drinking
the enlightened water.

BORROWED LIGHT

Three Maries at the sepulchre –
insolent light
on a blue lintel.

No soft focus –
chemical messengers
have silica in their wings

the hot specifics
from some occurrence
outside the picture

a tree
in quiet landscape
becoming radiant.

BYSTANDER AT THE VISITATION

I first saw them
as figures without a context –
but as they embraced
in the silence
between one utterance
and another

I glimpsed
Mary and Elisabeth,
the action of sunlight
on dew,
their unborn children,
innocent of syntax,

listening in.

Andrew Staniland

MEETING

For two human beings mysteriously
       and unexpectedly to meet,
To stand face to face, completely still,
       and through each otherness,
           each lost unknowingness,
To learn attentive love
– To build, like Blake's golden builders,
       a sacred dwelling place
           of listening and truth,
Celebrate in it a profanely playful,
       constantly changing communion,
           as innocent as brave,
An intimacy far deeper
       than familiarity –
For two human beings to meet
       and simply be themselves,
           really willing to be loved,
For such a state of grace, such a miracle
       to happen in this world,
What wonders must we accomplish,
       what other miracles first?
Though only something so simple,
       simple as Brahman itself,
           could be so difficult for us.

What an intricacy of chances,
       coincidental fates,
What transits of Venus or Saturn,
       initiate the moment
           that passes in a nervous dream, unless,
Ready somehow, we wake
       to our full loneliness?
But how many doubtful, reluctant ghosts,
       till the telling of their story sets them free,
Mutely deny our hearts,

to their own sorrow too?
Fossilised strata of long-dead lives
         our bodies need to break through
– A soldier's panic, suspended in slaughter,
Or an eleventh century cleric's
         religious hatred of women,
A demon's rejection of love.

And all these are the child, the bruised survivor
         of the journey through giant land,
Whose makeshift suit of armour
         we've grown too big to need
                  but still feel safe inside,
Whose battles we keep fighting
         for fear of repetition.
Only the child can heal the child. How else
         can we ever change the past
                  into eternity?

How many masks have to peel from the face
         for true transparency?
All the layers of forbidden emotion,
         the lineaments of ridiculed desire:
Now a permanent frown or ticking nerve,
         a rigid cheek or jaw,
Or an anxious, sexless expression,
         forlornly seeking erotic peace,
                  the redemption of the body.

What persuades a bitter mouth
         to release its succulence,
Or the eyes' opacity
         to shine like pure, deep wells
                  of personality,
Or the choked and guilty voice
         to cry at last and sing
                  its own original song?

In the sky invisible armies
         of angels and demons fight,
Swirling like clouds of smoke and light,
         or the final spiritual battle
                  in the Ramayana,

And the Earth seems to feel the shock
      of a sudden conjunction of feelings
           like the tearing of a veil.

But the night itself is clear, the rising moon,
      icy and bright,
           makes the dark street phosphorescent,
And the glittering choir of stars,
      like tears in the winter wind,
           hums, too high to hear,
To the growling, restless city.

The truth is, no more miracles are needed
      than these, which we are too,
           for such a meeting,
Only more patient heartwork,
      faith in our fruitfulness,
Till we know, till we feel for real,
      why love is right,
The simple paradox of unity.

Kenneth Steven

PEARLS

They were the reason the Romans came here –
River things, spun into milky globes over years and years.
I often wonder who it was who found them first,
Those mussels, dark shells whorled and folded
Like hands in prayer, embedded in feet of shingle.

The travellers knew where they were. The unsettled people
Who followed the seasons, the stars, yearned only the open road.
They carried the knowledge of pearls inside them, secret,
Could tell the very bend of river each pearl had come from –
This one like the pale globe of Venus at dawn,
This one a skylark's egg, and this the blush of a young girl's lips.

Yet the Romans never reached the Highland rivers
Where the best pearls sleep. They were kept out
By the painted people, the Pictish hordes
Bristling on the border like bad weather.

The pearls outlived even the travellers, whose freedom
Was bricked into the big towns long enough ago,
Who did not understand any longer
The language of the land.

In the last part of the north
In the startling blue of the rivers
The shells still grow. Their pearls are stories
That take a hundred years to tell.

HER MORNING

It has rained for days –
Choirs have sung from roofs and windows,
The lanes are knee-deep in November.

But this morning, this Sunday morning,
The rain glitters in mica
When sunlight opens like a bud across the fields.

Once upon a time it snowed in mid-November –
Great soft kittens' paws of snow that spun
Out of a grey-dark sky until
The house crouched more than silent,
Like some gigantic snowball in the woods.
He came and asked if she would go for holly.

Half-dark the woods, the stars like seeds,
Pale in a frightened sky. She holds his hand –
He smells of pipesmoke, moss, old books and cloth –
And suddenly he is her father
And she is six years old
Her sledge thudding at her back, her feet too small.

The holly cuts their hands with shiny spines,
Those berries the same colour as the beads
That bleed their fingers. At last
Her hands are wounds, all red and raw,
Yet never in her life before
Has she felt so alive.

All that was a flock of winters back –
The years have flown like swallows, lifted one on one
And stretched into the darkness of the past.
Only his photograph is left, frozen black and white,
A smile that might be crying –
A broken ledge of time.

Now the whole house echoes
With her aloneness. He never said goodbye;
How does one ever grieve enough for one who's gone?
The rain is washing him away,
And in the end the river finds the sea, the journey's done –
And all the world is salt.

She goes downstairs and hears the rain has stopped.
The church bells bloom across the fields
And suddenly a gust of sun blows through the trees;
She cannot see, she's blinded by the light –

For a moment she can feel his arms about her,
The dance that whirled her heart.

She breathes his name and he is gone,
And yet she feels his smile
So close it stills her cheek.
She starts towards his absence
Like broken glass-shattered fragments
Refracted by the light.

Sally Thompson

TROUBADOUR

If I send you broken words
will you make them rhyme
will you collect their scattered thoughts
and make them into mine

Will you gather up the shards
of meanings I've mislaid
and tenderly, assemble them
in forms I would have made

If I send you fractured rhythms
will you make them whole
and find for me the song that longs
to pour out of my soul

Will you listen through the silence
for the hopes I cannot see
and weaving them in coloured patterns
give them back to me

If I send you tarnished verses
will you make them glow
and polish them into the dreams
I may not dare to know

Will you offer me your hand
to write, when mine grows weak
and hear the message I would send
in words I cannot speak

AWAKENING

The light fell
opening a window of consciousness

The spirit woke
and looked up
shading its eyes

A tree dropped its hanging branches
deepening the shade

And in that dappled brightness
belief grounded itself

Held its shape for just long enough

Finally
the spirit

Leapt

THE RETURN

You have come again
breathed back
in the cradling of the wind

I might have missed you
were it not for the ocean's wave
riding the breeze behind you

I saw your light
glimmering
like a star in a snowstorm

A little hidden
but strong and true

And now you have returned
I can breathe again
take in the freshness of the air
the sweet smells of summer

And
reaching for your hand
touch
my
own

Lucy Trevitt

WE MAKE OUR PILGRIMAGE

We make our pilgrimage
on a small raft.
There is no medicine man
or stone goddess,
Only the quiet of Love
can do this now,
Holding back the clouds
to let the light shine through,
It is as necessary as breathing,
to die into the sunrise –
And through the cracks
we see her
and are changed.

SOPHIA'S SONG

Hers is the heart
hers is the pain
and hers is the eclipse
of the full moon,
the wisdom that rises
with the dew;
and all that remains of the night
is vanishing in her face
reflected into the pale sky –
She was the one
who first sang to me
the poetry of real life,
the light shining through the shadows,
and the tender conscience
that holds this sacred space
where the colours change.

TAKE MY TEARS

Take my tears,
they are the language of a new Love
and a new Life,
a place of no words
where my soul seeks it's echo
with truth.

No-one has told me these things before
and I am touched
by an infinite richness
and infinite pain
I know nothing of,
a place of opposites
deep and hidden
in the opening of my own heart.

All her life she's been trying to teach me
about trust, and fear,
and we must have courage
now that we have come so far,
these weeping voices have the after-image
of empathy
and are the ritual for change –

We must live for love
if we live at all.

WHEN WE REMEMBER

When we remember
        Who we really are
We are free.
Miracles wait not on time.
With roots like a tree
And wings like a butterfly,
I am still as God created me.

IF I COULD BE STILL

If I could be still,
If I could be in a place
without speaking, or thinking
without bargaining or blaming
or escaping into a comfortless oblivion,
without remembering, or hoping
or crying out numb inside,
If I could submerse myself
in the most absolute silence
then perhaps I could hear myself
in the limitless expanse
and be, beyond my knowing.

Daisy Tufnell

from THE THEORY OF POST-SOPHISTICATION

Data

What is done cannot be undone,
only unfolded,
leaving lines.
She spreads out the paper;
the flapping bird is gone.

What are they thinking about?
What are they thinking for?

She has forgotten what it is like
to walk through the grass and be unhappy.
She has forgotten the sensation
of believing she needs to Believe.

There are meadows, on the slope below the wood,
of Quaking Grass, Pignut and Cat's Ear,
Slow Worms, Jay's Feathers and Marbled Whites.
How is it possible to avoid this?
How is it possible
not to be alive?

Dark shadows hang below the trees.
Cows move slowly.

Saliva swells in her mouth
bejewelling the meetings of her lips.
She tastes the air,
thick with pollen and pollution,
her lungs heavy,
her body tired.
How can she explain this state of Bliss?

People do not want to unfold.

She is not without compassion;
how can she be
when the light is everywhere?

I see what lies in folds,
is trapped in pockets
of sophisticated paper;
I am marked by memories
of a Flapping Bird.

I am a creased sheet
worn thin with unfolding,
light penetrating the perforations
that mark the person
who I thought I was.

She can do nothing
but smooth herself out
over the arc of the globe,
stretching her spine on the hard ridge
of the world's back.

Once,
her unfolding was a journey
and she trod a Way with words.

Now,
I am weary of words,
tired of the folding and unfolding
that words evoke.

Once
she was able to see
the mountains and valleys
and feel the sorrows
trapped and released
as Paper ripped
and sellotape sealed the loss.
She was a Flapping Bird,
a Diamond Base;

venerated for her bright wings
and gimlet eyes:
the Hawk and the Eagle,
the Kingfisher, bright and blue,
above the water,
looping behind the trees,
again and again,
sure of her Form.

She played with words
and thought-knives
until her Bird unravelled,
and her companions
unfolded
or fled;
mostly they fled.

She watched as
Lilies turned to Frogs or Dancing Cranes.
And always
the final unfolding avoided;
always the questions:
what am I supposed to be?
what is my Form?
where is my Beloved?

The folding of paper.

She has seen a Clean Sheet
who folded and unfolded himself
only for others;
it is why she is as she is
now.

If I could show you how bright the marigolds are
nothing would matter.

Marigolds catching sunlight,
moving fractionally from side to side,
heat hazed at the tips of their overlapping,
tilted towards a cloud covered sun,
petals.

In one moment,
one pure moment,
looking,
only looking.
Once seen, always seen.
Ripping time open,
cut bare into Orange.

Just marigolds.
This is how it always is:
beauty, pain, existence and passion.
Just Marigolds.
Everything to be seen;
not with the effort of concentration,
nor through analysis,
(though this may take you close),
but by not being afraid;
by unfolding, accepting;
not asking or demanding or seeking anything.
Not avoiding.
Especially not avoiding.
Marigolds.

Just Marigolds.

As soon as she writes
she is limited.
She becomes an observer of herself.

No. There is another ...

Pen on paper.
Laughter deep in the belly
bubbling;
light twirling and twisting,
Bliss like water over soft- mossed stone.
Bright.
So bright.

Sun burning my retina
from the window, rich with garden beyond.
Nectar veined.

Nectar full-flowered.
Sweetness in my legs,
rising and throbbing in my limbs,
my gut full of honeyed joy;
the surface tired;
Body-mind, ego, whatever,
thin and fragile,
taut over the layer of white brightness,
living its creased life.

Pools of blue and green.
Who is the fool now?
Who is the dance?

This is her creased self
generated
by circumstance of being here.

This is my creased self
thin as tissue,
in a world of flapping birds.

Hypothesis

Today she is not well:
her world spins,
her limbs ache ,
her hormones weep,
and her head thuds
but....

This is not what it is about.
This is never what it is about.

She cannot avoid the fact
that, first and forever,
she is un-moved.

The nascent joy of every moment
dances through my being
beyond the dis-ease.

What is true does not change;
only the manifestation.
Perhaps the paper can transform?

Her mouth moves unknowing;
what words will come
out of Consciousness?

Love. Real. Tangible. Passionate?
Alive?

She is bursting with un-thought thoughts.

Light:
zigzagging, undulating, across a black velvet cosmos;
fantastic Fourier Transforms,
streams and strings,
the lyre and the star and the Great Voice
contracted
To spirit and flesh.

Light:
full throttled,
bliss turning and whirling
reduced to form
Only if I wish :
only
at this time.

There is a moment when her eyes cease to look,
when they become points
through which light registers,
when there is no difference between looking and seeing,
between the flower that is looked at
and the woman who looks.

I rest like a cat
in a sun spattered garden
Purring in silence.

HOME

I have been stripped:
skin peeled again and again
until I am not raw but bright.
There is no escape from pain or pleasure,
nor can I be insensible to beauty
or the Sorrows of the World.
I have no parry
for the soft blow to the heart
or the hard blow to the bone;
flesh bruises with velvet or steel.
Yesterday I stood on the edge of my self
in a balancing act between ether and earth,
walking a tightrope
afraid in case I flew or fell.
Now I am stripped of excuses and reasons,
lying on the bare earth, feeling my body merging
with a scale sloughing dragon,
a resurrecting Christ, a bright sphere of Beauty,
Paradise regained.

Philip Wells

ALREADY

"Live as though the time were here" Neitzsche

It's already here

The silver web of silence glows like mercury
And in your ear the swallows shriek in the soft rain
Above the temple bells humming like starlight
And inside, like a golden bullet fired inside a speeding
Golden bullet, the spirit moves faster than science

It's already here

In my pocket enough power to turn a city of love
Into little pieces of people falling like leaves of blood,
In my heart enough love to split my body
Into many parts, that my neighbour may die,
That my neighbours may be free

It's already here

The children play in a paradise of money
Where they grow and grow and vote for fame;
Or the sudden silver of the hidden water
Where the child dives into the world
That God sees too

It's already here

Our fingers speaking in tongues
Our bodies trembling with the invisible
Curtains opening in the desert city
Windows opening in the desert city
We are walking in a wind

It's already here

Our wings are not moving yet we are carried
Our wings are moving and we can dip and turn
And dance in this wind, we can see the valleys of a breeze
And the mountain ranges of the breath, breathing
To be God's everywhere and all at once

It's already here

FIRE

"The heart is nothing but a sea of fire" Rumi

Hypnosis dances your eyes
back to the beginning.
The lone candle flares
its last golden message:
There is a love
that burns us into love.

Fire changes everything.
The darkness cowers, breathes
its last ashen breath,
for we can suspend fire
like suns for more lives
than we can think of.

The stars shine into your heart:
they never let you forget
that you burn to be like them.
Though darkness must come again,
when your doubt is deep enough
all the suns will pour back in.

Hands will not blister
when they touch you, but long to be
the supernova you have become,
in your eyes, your slow grace:

you walked through hell: all are
aghast at your unburned lips –

the lips of a child that breathed
whatever was, and the world became.
In the swift hands of the wind
or the curled palm of the waves
the world became, and the child in you
stood naked by the shore.

You walked through the deep burning
gardens, singing of the Age of Fire, listening
to the fire that roars now in your soul.
Everything is there; or *here*; between the syllables,
Beyond the whispers of meaning;
A new love burning in the silence.

EASTBOURNE CLIFFS

Further, further, Daddy

My little boy takes me further in the sun
Into a miracle where the white pebble
Sits in the chapel of a spring
By the white, white cliffs

And the trickle of the water
Is a rhythm of love:
It is love calling,
This water falling:

Further, further, Daddy

This water falling
On the white pebble
I place now in the secret box
I carry with me forever

For this is the same
White pebble
My son places
On my grave

Further, further, Daddy

And I can hear him clear
As a spring in the white cliff
From the far place
Where I cannot touch him

But where our listening,
Despite all the deep divides,
Splashes us together in the great light
In an everlasting wave of love.

Lynne Wycherley

OUT OF THE SKY

We wake to snowfall, slow-motion, hypnotic,
a bright poem falling out of the sky
like god sleeting through the world

and time dissolving. Fibre-glass falling
on roof-tree and wall, ash-branch and bole,
just glacial in each leaf's valley

as mercury floats on zero and the short day
utters ice. Hexagons, no two the same,
white words that will never be spoken again.

We watch their crystals haunt and glow
and for one breath we see our lives
as burning, brief, miraculous as snow.

ISLAND LIGHT

Moments so bright they are visionary –

miraculous fish
slipping through our hands –

Eynhallow
in its dazzling rösts,

Papay in terns' wings,
a trembling cloth,

Stronsay suspended
on sapphire

before the brief light
steals away

and we're left on
a hesistant shore-line

deftly caught
in impalpable nets

our love, our dreams, our pain.

röst – tidal race

APPLE BLOSSOM

No words pure enough
to speak this tree, its scented
white poem, light's silk.

Is a life long enough to learn
its language, inextricable branches,
its thousand routes into sky?

See: its stars are not pinned
to unreachable boughs,
the burn of the absolute blue

but float, whisper-close, in wild
aromas. I breathe and see
the universe through its heaven

and the blossom makes a bride of me,
snows on my skin. Marries
me to the world again

the fragrant and the green,
the longed-for return
as grain by crushed grain

the heart's stored pain crumbles.
Hardpan dissolving
in blossom, light's kiss.

WOMAN AND WATER

Don't ask me to choose
between near and far,
light on the water,
the breeze in your hair,
your midland vowels just held
between malt and honey.

Here on the quay
your presence brings
a timbre, breath, and touch;
across the fetch
the isles are hung with cobalt,
heaven-wrapped

so I am balanced
between two joys,
the warmth in your eyes,
the sea's largesse,
its gift of
unbearable brightness.

A MENHIR FOR THE CATHARS

after the sculpture by J.Severac

Not for you the tortured cross,
fetters of pain, only flight, ascension,

a core of blue, this keyhole cut through
in the outline of a dove

235 Into The Further Reaches 235

as if love could pierce the densest rock
or wings have air when the world crushes.

You fled to your nests, cliff fortresses –
Quéribus, Montsegur, Puylaurens,

a transhumance where no grass grows
while blood-knights climbed the valleys

with their brands. To burn you, flesh to bone,
and the war of the heart not won.

Now absence evokes you, the wash
of the wind, slant light on bare stone,

high walls that know the wingbeats of the stars.
In my heart I might glimpse you:

I close my eyes and see faint snow –
white doves, the inviolable blue.

Biographies

Peter Abbs

Professor of Creative Writing at the University of Sussex, Peter has been engaged for many years with the teaching of literature and the nature of aesthetic education. He has written widely on arts education and Socratic learning, and has published seven volumes of poetry. He has lectured on education and given poetry readings in Europe, Australia, India and the USA. His two most recent books are *Against the Flow: Education, the Arts and Postmodern Culture* (Routledge Falmer, 2003) and *Viva La Vida* (Salt, 2004)

www.peterabbs.co.uk

Shanta Acharya

Born in India, educated at Oxford and Harvard, Shanta currently lives in London. Her publications include *Shringara* (Shoestring Press, UK; 2006), *Looking In, Looking Out,* (Headland Publications, UK; 2005) *Numbering Our Days' Illusions* (Rockingham Press, UK; 1995) where 'Not One of the Myths' appears, and *Not This, Not That* (Rupa & Co, India; 1994) where 'Day of Reckoning' appears. She is working on her next collection, where 'The Wishing Tree' will appear.

www.shantaacharya.com

Roselle Angwin

Roselle has been described as 'a poet of the bright moment... whose own source of creative inspiration is her native West Country, the Scottish islands, and a highly individual blend of Celtic mythology, psychology, shamanic transformation and Buddhist thinking.' She is also an author, course facilitator and painter. She lives in South Devon.

www.fire-in-the-head.co.uk

William Ayot

William delivers seminars and workshops on leadership, communication and personal impact to organisations around the world using poetry and story to revivify the workplace. Writing includes *The Water Cage*, his latest collection *Small Things that Matter* and the play *Bengal Lancer* (Leicester & London). He lives near Chepstow.

www.oliviermythodrama.com

Sebastian Barker

Chair of the Poetry Society 1988 to 1992; Fellow of the Royal Society of Literature from 1997; Editor of *The London Magazine* from 2002. *Guarding the Border: Selected Poems* (Enitharmon 1992); *The Dream of Intelligence* (Littlewood Arc 1992); *Damnatio Memoriae: Erased from Memory* (Enitharmon 2004); *The Matter of Europe* (Menard Press 2005); *The Erotics of God* (Smokestack Books 2005).

www.thelondonmagazine.net

Matthew Barton

Matthew's books include *Learning To Row* (Peterloo, 1999), and *The Winding Road* an anthology of poems for parents and children (Hawthorn Press 2004). He has won a large number of awards for his work, including BBC Wildlife Poet of the Year, an Arts Council Writer's Award, a Hawthornden Fellowship, and 2nd. prize in the National Poetry Competition. Currently he works as translator and editor and a poetry tutor on Bristol University's creative writing diploma. He lives with his family in Bristol.

Claudine Whiting Bloomfield

Born 1971 in Norfolk, though much of her early life was spent in the United States, Claudine holds an honours degree in Literature and received a Fellowship for Excellence in English in 1993. She found her voice as a poet returning to England in 1998, and her work has appeared in magazines and anthologies. Claudine lives in Nailsworth, Gloucestershire with her husband and children, and works as a writer and book editor.

Peter Brennan

Having recently retired from the role of Head of English at one of London's leading schools, Peter Brennan is pursuing a new career as a freelance tutor and publisher. He leads courses in literature and spirituality, and his collection *Torch of Venus* is available from Perdika Press, London.

www.perdikapress.com

Richard Burns

Born in London in 1943, into a family of musicians, Richard's poems have been translated into 20 languages. Recent books include *Against Perfection* (1999), *Croft Woods* (1999), *The Manager* (2001), *Book With No Back Cover* (2003), *Avebury* (e-book, 2003), and *For the Living* (2004). In 2005, he was awarded the international Morava Poetry Prize for *In a Time of Drought* (2006). An early draft of 'The Blue Butterfly' (2006) received the Wingate-Jewish Quarterly Award for Poetry. He lives in Cambridgeshire.

www.richardburns.eu

David Caddy

Edits *Tears in the Fence* literary magazine and is a freelance English Studies and writing tutor. He recently started thewordtravels.com, organising literary holidays and writing breaks. His latest books are *The Willy Poems* (Clamp Down Press 2004) and *City of Words* (Blue Island Publishing 2006). He lives near Blandford Forum.

www.tearsinthefence.co.uk

Anne Cluysenaar

Born Brussels 1936; graduate of Trinty College, Dublin; lives in Wales. *Nodes* (1971), *Double Helix* (1982), *Timeslips, New and Selected Poems* (1997). Forthcoming in 2008: a book-length sequence on the Monmouth-born naturalist Alfred Russell Wallace. With support from the Welsh Academi, Anne is now focussing on the geneology and paleontology of Wales.

Lisa Dart

Lecturer in Education at the University of Sussex for ten years, Lisa has published work on education, creativity and the imagination. Currently, she is Head of Curriculum Enhancement at St Bede's school and is completing her doctorate on poetry and post-modernism. Her debut pamphlet *The Self in the Photograph* was published last year. She lives in Eastbourne.

Owen Davis

Owen, who has lived in Dorset for many years, has published 13 books of poems, two cassettes of poetry and music and a collection on CD, *Out There*, with music by Cathy Stevens, Charles Dickie and Frank Perry.

David Donaldson

David has spent most of his working life in education, in both the state and independent sectors. He now lives in Herefordshire and has been teaching in the Steiner School in Much Dewchurch for the past fifteen years. He has published collections, each part financed by subscition.

Diana Durham

Author of the non-fiction *The Return of King Arthur* (Tarcher/Penguin 2004) and two poetry collections: *Sea of Glass* (The Diamond Press, 1990) and *To the End of the Night* (Northwoods Press, winner of their 2003 competition). In the UK, Diana worked with the Angels of Fire performance group. In New Hampshire she founded the state funded '3 Voices' – three women writers who perform state-wide.

www.dianadurham.net

Aidan Andrew Dun

Aidan spent a fantastical childhood in the West Indies and knew his calling for poetry from an early age. Returning to London as a teenager, he travelled globally for more than a decade before writing his first epic poem *Vale Royal* (Goldmark, 1995) which, launched at the Royal Albert Hall, earned him the title Poet of Kings Cross. His second epic *Universal* (Goldmark, 2002) was launched at City Lights, San Francisco. *The Uninhabitable City* (Goldmark 2005), a collection of short poems, was launched at the Gymnasium in Kings Cross. He is currently at work on a third epic.

www.aidandun.com

Marion Fawlk

Marion is a poet and visual artist although like Mallarmé she sees no difference between the visual and the poetic, all are hierolglyphs of the soul. Work has been performed at St. Martin in the Fields with composer Rosemary Duxbury and at other festivals in the U.K. as well as in the sacred city of Fez, Morocco, with images celebrating Islamic life. Her poems appeared in *Earth Ascending* (Stride, 1997.) She lives in Stroud.

Carolyn Finlay

Carolyn's poetry appears in magazines and anthologies including *Earth Ascending* (Stride 1995), *Earth Songs* (Green Books 2002) and *The Book of Hopes and Dreams* (Bluechrome 2006). She has published two poetry books, *Giveaway* (Stride 1996) and *Foreigner* (Waterdog Press 2001), and a short story, 'Zoom', in *Necrologue* (Diva Books 2003). She lives in Cheltenham.

Rose Flint

An award winning poet, Rose is also an art therapist. She teaches creative writing and uses the therapeutic power of poetry in her work as a writer in healthcare, in hospitals and the community. She has three collections: *Blue Horse of Morning* (Seren) *Firesigns* (Poetry Salzburg) and *Nekyia* (Stride, 2005). She lives in Bath.

Cora Greenhill

Cora's poetry is widely published, and she has two collections, *Dreadful Work* and *Deep in Time*. She recently moved to Crete, following the labyrinth that has led her there as a pilgrim and as a teacher of Gabrielle Roth's dancework for many years, and is now crafting a collection of her Cretan writing.

www.thirteenthmoon.co.uk

David H.W. Grubb

Born 1941. David's most recent poetry collections are *The Elephant In The Room* (Driftwood) and *Out of the Marvellous* (Oleander, 2006). Recently compiled *Sounding Heaven and Earth* (Canterbury Press). Tutor of Creative Writing at the River and Rowing Museum, Henley on Thames. Tutor in Creative Writing at Reading University.

Geoffrey Godbert

Geoffrey has had fourteen poetry collections published and his *Collected Poems* are expected in 2007. He is co-editor of two Faber poetry anthologies and editor of an anthology of prose poems. Of his work, Harold Pinter comments: 'Geoffrey will certainly end up with the poets in heaven.' He lives in Somerset.

Jill Haas

Jill Haas is an American writer whose credits include: *America-America*, a dramatic poem broadcast on Radio 4; *An Encyclopedia of Love*, a memoir published by Picador, USA; *The Last Days*, a 65-page poem published by Ripostes, Italy and a two-act play, *Bringing Up Baby*, a winner at the Watermill Playhouse's 2004 new writing competition. She lives in Oxford.

Keith Hackwood

Born in 1971 in Newport, South Wales. His interests include the integration of Hermetic and Vajrayana themes within poetry, the ongoing development of community based creativity (through Newport Archetypalists) and creating accessible forms for experiencing compassionate connection to the basic ground of human being. His three poems in this collection are from *100 Sonnets of Galactic Love* (PS Avalon, 2005). His first collection was *Charon's Hammer* (PS Avalon, 2005).

www.llanthewyroad.com/keith/about.html

Stephen Hall

Stephen was born and has lived all his life in London and has worked for many years in part time auxiliary psychiatric nursing. Other interests apart from poetry: writing and singing songs, meditation, and the Tao of everyday 21st century life.

Alyson Hallett

Alyson's first collection of poems will be published by Peterloo Poets in 2007. She has published a book of short stories *The Heart's Elliptical Orbit* (Solidus Press), written for Radio 4 and has a poem carved into Milsom Street pavement in Bath. She is currently writer-in-residence at The Small School in Hartland, Devon.

Adam Horovitz

Born in 1971 in London and bred in Gloucestershire, has been writing poetry for as long as he can remember. Since his early twenties, he has financed this by doing a variety of jobs, including silver service waiter, sheep dipper, journalist and barman. He lives in Stroud.

Libby Houston

Libby currently lives in Bristol working as a botanist of cliffs and gorges. *Cover of Darkness*, Selected Poems 1961-1998 (Slow Dancer Press 1999) contains unexpected insights of four decades that began out loud in a Beatnik cellar; *Tam Lin and other tales* (Greville Press, 2005) reprints three of her narrative poems for children.

Alan Jackson

Born 1938. Very active on reading scene in sixties and seventies, working with such as Adrian Mitchell and Brian Patten. Retired later from literary life to attend to matters down in the abyss. Books: *Penguin Modern Poets 12*, *The Grim Wayfarer* (Fulcrum Press), *The Guardians Arrive, Heart of the Sun, Salutations* (Collected Poems, Polygon), *Love, Death and Angel*. Has lived for many years in Edinburgh.

Norman Jope

Norman was born in Plymouth, where he now lives again after lengthy periods in other locations (most recently Swindon, Bristol and Budapest). His collection *For The Wedding-Guest* was published by Stride in 1997, and his work has appeared in a wide range of publications in Britain and beyond.

Georgina Yael Johnson

Georgina was born in Sheffield in 1967 and now lives in Israel. After years in the wilderness, with passing phases as an investigative journalist and copywriter, engagement in spiritual healing, meditation and psychic development led her back to the promised land of poetry. Fascinated by connections between creativity and spiritual growth, she is presently completing her first collection: *Ways to Eden.*

www.geocities.com/veratherapy

Nora Leonard

In addition to articles on dreamwork and astrology, Nora has had poems published in magazines and anthologies. She has examined paradigms of spirituality on the Ealing Grid for Learning. She has written a screenplay (yet to be produced), and is currently working on a novel. She lives in West London.

www.mythicmaps.net

Grevel Lindop

Grevel lives in Manchester, where he was formerly a Professor of English at the University. His six books of poems include *Selected Poems* (2000) and *Playing With Fire* (2006), both from Carcanet. He has edited work by De Quincey, Chatterton and Robert Graves, and contributes to many literary journals.

www.grevel.co.uk

Rupert M Loydell

Rupert is Lecturer in Creative Writing at University College Falmouth, the Managing Editor of Stride Publications, Editor of Stride magazine, and a regular contributor of articles and reviews to Tangents magazine. Recent publications include *A Conference of Voices, The Museum of Light* and *Endlessly Divisible*, and four collaborative works. *The Smallest Deaths* was recently published by Bluechrome (2005).

www.stridemagazine.co.uk

Janis Mackay

Janis was born in Edinburgh and after years working as a voice teacher and storyteller she recently completed an MA in creative writing and personal development at the University of Sussex. She writes about the land and is inspired by a sense of place and experiences poetry and speaking poetry as a way of dwelling - in language, herself and the land.

Kevan Manwaring

Kevan is a poet, storyteller, novelist and teacher living in Bath, and has been performing his poetry and stories for over a decade in venues across Britain. In 1998 he was awarded the Bardic Chair of Caer Badon. He is the author of *The Long Woman*, a novel (Awen 2004), and *The Bardic Handbook* (Gothic Image 2006). He teaches creative writing for the Open University and freelance workshops in writing and performance.
www.druidnetwork.org/profiles/people/kevan_manwaring.html

Ruth Marshall

Ruth was born in Glasgow in 1956, grew up in East Kilbride, and moved to Co. Clare, Ireland in 1986 where she now lives. Single parent of Iain. Editor of *Network Ireland* holistic magazine since 1995. Author of *Celebrating Irish Festivals* (Hawthorn Press, 2003). She has poetry published in journals and anthologies in UK and Ireland.

Paul Matthews

Paul is a lecturer at Emerson College, in Sussex. *The Ground that Love Seeks* (Five Seasons Press) is a book of his poems. *Sing Me the Creation* (Hawthorn Press) is an inspirational book for Creative Writing. He is the Founder of Poetry OtherWise, a week-long summer gathering held at Emerson College since 2000.

Anne Brayton Meek

Born in Suffolk, Anne lives in London. Ran Piccadilly Poets at Jermyn Street Theatre during 1990's, Sir George Trevelyan was patron. Teaches singing and voice – also performs. Does home visits. Belongs to Temenos Academy. On team at St. Ethelburga's Centre for peace and reconciliation. One poetry publication, and has published poems in various magazines.

Jehanne Mehta

Born 1941. Jehanne is a singer, songwriter, poet. She has written poems since childhood, songs since her twenties. Four poetry books published and five albums of songs recorded, of which the latest, *Emblem*, came out in 2006. Married with three grown up children and living in Stroud, Gloucestershire with her husband and musical partner, Rob.

Gabriel Bradford Millar

Gabriel Bradford Millar has been a therapist with maladjusted and handicapped teenagers for over 20 years. She has taught English and given over 80 poetry readings and playshops (Down from the Ivory Tower). Her work is distilled into *The Saving Flame* (Five Seasons Press, 2001). She lives in Stroud.

Fiona Owen

Fiona is the author of *Imagining the Full Hundred* and *O My Swan*. She also co-writes and performs music with Gorwel Owen, and teaches literature, humanities and creative writing for the Open University. She has recently completed *Going Gentle* and is writing *No Endless Earth*, a book of ecocritical essays. She lives on Anglesey.

www.rhwng.com

Rosemary Palmeira

Rosemary lives in Beverley, E Yorks. She is a writer and poet and has had many works published in journals and anthologies. She edited *In the Gold of Flesh – Poems of Birth & Motherhood* (The Women's Press. 1990). She works variously as a writer, teacher, social worker and psychotherapist and currently leads creative writing, drama and art workshops with asylum seekers. She is married with three children.

Will Parfitt

Born 1950, Will lives in Glastonbury, England, and is the author of several non-fiction books which have been translated into more than ten languages. A Kabbalist and psychotherapist, he is the director of PS Avalon. Will's earliest recalled poem was written over forty years ago, and he has published a selection of poems since then titled *Through The Gates of Matter* (PS Avalon, 2003). Will's most recent publications are *Kabbalah for Life* (Rider, 2006) and *The Parfait Amour Tarot* (Hermatena, 2006)

www.willparfitt.com

Mario Petrucci

Mario secured the Arvon prize with *Heavy Water: a poem for Chernobyl* (Enitharmon), described as 'instructive, moving and aesthetically admirable' by Vernon Scannell. He has run key residencies at the Imperial War Museum and BBC Radio 3. *Fearnought: poems for Southwell Workhouse* (National Trust) presents a remarkable combination of history, photography and poetry. He lives in London.

mariopetrucci.port5.com

Louise Amelia Phelps

Louise Amelia is an artist and writer from London. She completed her degree in sculpture from Bath Spa University College in 2000. Since then she has exhibited in Cairo, New York and California. Her written work has been published in childrens books and magazines in the UK and Holland while personal readings of her stories continue to enchant young and old.

www.thedreamingpages.com

Jennie Powell

Born in Glasgow, Jennie migrated to London in her twenties. Throughout an unremarkable working life she was always drawn home to spirit and community. Her home kept getting larger; it still does. Her first poetry collection, *The Grain in the Wood*, was published by The Lotus Foundation (2004). She now lives in Cheltenham.

Jay Ramsay

Editor of this and several other anthologies, Jay is a poet, psychotherapist and healer. Project director of *Chrysalis—the poet in you* (since 1990) with its two part course by post, he is the author, co-author and editor of over 30 books including *The Heart's Ragged Evangelist* – love poems for the greater love (PS Avalon, 2005). He is currently poet in residence at St James' Church, Piccadilly, London. He lives in Stroud.

www.lotusfoundation.org.uk/jayramsay

Angie Rawlinson

Angie's poetry seeks to challenge our feminine and masculine identity. She is in search of a raw and reflective language for the self that she often calls 'The cry within the I'. She has written in cities across the world and now lives in Forest Row, Sussex on the edge of the Ashdown Forest.

www.angierawlinsonpoetry.co.uk

Ben Rayner

Ben has a background as a professional skydiver, travelling worldwide. He is also a massage therapist and healer, practices deep meditation, and receives Spirit, Energy and Survival skills teachings from the Apache, Maori and Inuit. He is currently teaching workshops, working as a healer, recording an album of piano music, and enjoying life immensely.

Peter Redgrove

Peter died in 2003. In his lifetime he published many volumes of poetry, novels, and non-fiction works. He wrote many radio plays, one of which, *Florent And The Tuxedo Millions*, won the Priz Italia. This year two final volumes of poetry appear: *A Speaker For The Silver Goddess* (Stride Publications) and *The Harper* (Jonathan Cape).

en.wikipedia.org/wiki/Peter_Redgrove

Dee Rimbaud

Dee is a poet, novelist, artist, spiritual healer and new age hobo. He is currently eschewing fixed abodes for a life of freedom and beauty. Publications include the award winning *Dropping Ecstasy With The Angels* and *Stealing Heaven From The Lips Of God* (Bluechrome Publishing).

Alan Rycroft

Alan was born in London in 1957, grew up in Brighton and studied English Literature at the University of East Anglia. He trained as a college lecturer and has an MA in Applied Linguistics. As well as teaching in the UK and Europe he has taught English in universities and companies in North Africa, the Middle East and China, Thailand and Korea. His first major collection is in preparation.

Henry Shukman

Henry 's collection, *In Dr No's Garden*, won the Aldeburgh Poetry Prize 2003 and was a Book of the Year in the (London) Times and Guardian. His poems have appeared in the Guardian, Times, Daily Telegraph, Independent on Sunday, T.L.S., London Review of Books and New Republic. He has worked as a travelwriter and a trombonist. He lives in Santa Fe, New Mexico.

Karen Eberhardt Shelton

Karen lived in the U.S. for many years, now permanently in England. A vegetarian poet/writer all her life, associate editor of *Green Fuse* (California) for 5 years, on Moor Poets committee (Dartmoor), co-author of *The Message* with Jay Ramsay (David Paul 2002), previously a newspaper columnist, longing to heal the earth. A new anthology edited by Karen titled *A Women's Guide to Saving the World* is due out from The Book Guild during 2007.

Penelope Shuttle

Penelope lives in Cornwall, is the widow of Peter Redgrove, and has a grown-up daughter, Zoe. Shuttle has published six collections of poetry since 1980, three of which have been Poetry Book Society Recommendations. She co-authored, with Peter Redgrove, the pioneer study of menstruation, *The Wise Wound*, and its sequel *Alchemy For Women*. Her latest collection is *Redgrove's Wife* (Bloodaxe, 2006)

Pauline Stainer

Pauline's *The Lady and the Hare: Selected Poems* (Bloodaxe 2003), now in its second impression, was a Poetry Book Society Recommendation. After living in the Orkney Isles for some years, she is now in Suffolk.

Andrew Staniland

Andrew is an English writer, born in 1959 and currently living in London. He has published 2 novels, *The Beauty Of Psyche*, a retelling of the Greek myth, performed by actors against a backdrop of classical paintings, and *The Weight Of Light*, a description of a contemporary woman's spiritual practice. He has also published a Selected Poems, Three Narrative Poems and Four Plays.

www.andrewstaniland.co.uk

Kenneth Steven

Kenneth was born in Scotland in 1968. A melding of the landscape, stories, people and faith of Highland Scotland have formed the backdrop to all his writing. Twenty of his books have been published; his best-known volumes of poetry are *The Missing Days*, *Iona*, *Wild Horses* and *Columba* (St Andrews Press).

www.kennethsteven.co.uk

Sally Thompson

Originally trained as a classical musician, Sally currently practises as a barrister, living and working in central London. She is also a mediator and a member of Lapidus. Writing poetry has been a part of her life for the past 3 years in connection with Poetry Otherwise (Emerson College) and The Lotus Foundation.

Lucy Trevitt

Born in 1970, Lucy is an artist and poet whose creative expression has emerged and developed as an inseparable part of a long and transformational journey with illness and disability. This has also been her spiritual training, and has brought some of the mysteries of existence into sharp focus. She works empathically and intuitively with these silent resources to attempt to give voice to the poetics of the unknown. She lives in Stroud.

Daisy Tufnell

She is a 45 year old gardener and clarity consultant living near Stroud who writes poetry in intense, sporadic bursts. For her, poetry is always an attempt to integrate and assimilate a multiplicity of truths. It is a process of spilling out a jumble of thoughts and honing them into something that resonates, not merely through words and patterns but through the spaces in between.

Philip Wells

Philip makes his living performing as The Fire Poet everywhere from 11 Downing Street to Westminster Abbey, from children's hospices and psychiatric units to maximum security prisons, from Newsnight to Radio 5 Live. Nothing, however, beats reciting Jabberwocky to a horde of three year olds wielding balloon swords. He lives in West London.

www.thefirepoet.com

Lynne Wycherley

Lynne lives in Oxfordshire, and works at Merton College. Widely published in journals, she was recently selected as an Alternative Generation Poet (Staple 2005). Her new collection *North Flight* (Shoestring Press) charts a lyrical journey from her birthplace near the Fens to Orkney, Shetland and Iceland.

Credits and Acknowledgements

Roselle Angwin: Out of Albion, Let It Be Enough Some Mornings and Taking Light all appear in Looking For Icarus (Bluechrome, 2005)

Sebastian Barker photo credit: John Minihan

Richard Burns: the following poems by have already been published: 'I will speak', 'Mosaic' and 'The wind's paths' in Book With no Back Cover, David Paul, London, 2003; 'The aeon lies torn in pieces' in The Manager, Elliott & Thompson, London, 2001; and the extract 'from Croft Woods' in Against Perfection, King of Hearts, Norwich, 1999, in Croft Woods, Lost Poetry Press, Cambridge, 1999, and in For the Living, Salt, Cambridge, 2004. Thanks to all the publishers.

Aidan Andrew Dun photo credit: Anastasia Alexander

Adam Horovitz photo © the Stroud News and Journal

Libby Houston "Gold" and "A Little Treachery" © Libby Houston 1999 from Cover of Darkness, Selected Poems 1961-1998, Slow Dancer Press (1999) by permission of the author
photo: Rosalind Grimshaw

Rupert M Loydell photo credit: Geoff Sutton

Fiona Owen: 'Because the Poet': the line 'hold this poem up to the light' is from a poem by John Powell Ward titled 'From a Phrase by Janet Montefiore' in A Certain Marvellous Thing (Seren, 1993); 'Door' was commended in the 'Sixth Scintilla Open Poetry Competition' and published in Scintilla 9; 'A Musing' published in O My Swan (Flarestack, 2003); 'Buddha-dog' published in Imagining the Full Hundred (Gwasg Pantycelyn, 2003)

Mario Petrucci photo credit: C. McNamee, 2005

Penelope Shuttle: photo credit: Caroline Forbes

Lynne Wycherley : "Island Light"*appears in North Flight Shoestring Press, 2006; "Out of the Sky" first appeared in Agenda, "Woman and Water" in Acumen, and "A Menhir for the Cathars" in Scintilla.

If any credits and acknowledgements have been omitted please let the publisher know and we will include them in any future editions of this anthology.

a selection of poetry books

Our purpose: to bring you the best new poetry with a psychospiritual content, to make poetry relevant, offering work that is contemplative and inspirational, with a dark, challenging edge.

The Heart's Ragged Evangelist   Jay Ramsay
ISBN: 0-9544764-7-6, 136 pp, Demi 8vo 140x216mm, £10.00

What does it mean for us to open to a greater love? Jay Ramsay's poems explore this theme personally and transpersonally within the context of a question he believes to be absolutely essential both to our present time and our future evolution. Jay explores this question and invites us into a mystery where we may discover we are much more interconnected than we know.

She Who Walks With Stones and Sings   Rachael Clyne
ISBN: 0-9544764-6-8, 112 pp, Demi 8vo 140x216mm, £10.00

Astonishingly rich poetry, full of spirit and humour, these poems touch the reader at the deepest level. Rachael draws much of her inspiration from nature and her love for the Goddess, as well as from her Jewish background, and uses poetry to express different aspects of the human journey: death and loss, family, relationships and she comments with humour on the challenges of aging.

Dead Leaves   Owen Ahrmanian
ISBN: 0-9544764-3-3, 152 pp, Demi 8vo 140x216mm, £10.00

Explore the redemptive possibilities which exist in the energy of bitterness. From voices of innocence and sweetness, through relationship-blocking contradictions, to an arche-typal, visionary root which nurtures energy into life, Ahrmanian's poems entice the reader towards a soulful resolution. Dare you risk it?

Charon's Hammer Keith Hackwood
ISBN: 0-9544764-2-5, 108 pp, Crown 189x246mm, £10.00

An opportunity to break bread and risk a tap dance with a man so in love with the world as to permit moonlight to sleep in his ears. Arch-druid of images, Hackwood tends and suckles the ugly and the beautiful alike with a metaphysician's fractal tenderness and a mother's devoted impunity. He just might change your life!

all these books plus our complete catalogue are available from Amazon and all good internet bookstores

for the fastest service and details of new and forthcoming titles please order your books at our website:

www.psavalon.com

PS AVALON

publishing with the spirit of inquiry

PS Avalon, Box 1865, Glastonbury, BA6 8YR, England.
email: info@psavalon.com
website: http://www.psavalon.com

PS Avalon Publishing is an independent and committed publisher offering a complete publishing service. As a small publisher enabled to take full advantage of the latest technological advances, PS Avalon Publishing can offer an alternative route for aspiring authors working in our particular fields of interest.

As well as publishing, PS Avalon offers an education programme that includes distance learning courses, groups, seminars, and other opportunities for personal and spiritual growth.

Whilst the nature of our work means we engage with people from all around the world, we are based in Glastonbury which is in the West Country of England.

Printed in the United Kingdom
by Lightning Source UK Ltd.
119832UK00001B/255-264